'My sport involves split-second timing and decision making, as well as the ability to stick with it. This book brilliantly illustrates how your mind really can triumph over matter.'

Frankie Dettori MBE, champion jockey

'A fascinating book about how we can be the architects of our own minds. Charlie makes a highly compelling case for the defining importance of temperament, mental poise and self-awareness to high performance – in any walk of life. And he tells us how to get there. A "must read" for anybody who wants to excel!'

General Sir Peter Wall, former Chief of General Staff of the British Army

'Charlie's *Inside Out* approach is immensely valuable. I have learned so much from the book.'

Lizzy Yarnold OBE, double Olympic champion

'*Inside Out* provides a very modern approach to personal leadership, packed with valuable insights blended from science, conventional wisdom and Charlie's own unique experience.'

David Nicol, former CEO, Brewin Dolphin

'Working with Charlie and his *Inside Out* approach was instrumental to my performances in Tokyo.'

Sophie Wells OBE, four-time Paralympic gold medallist

'Anyone interested in exploring their own performance potential is going to benefit immensely from this book.'

DS, former SAS squadron commander

'When it comes to performance psychology Charlie truly is an expert in his field. He played a huge role in helping me achieve my goal of becoming an Olympic champion.'

Kate French MBE, Olympic champion, Tokyo 2020

'This book provides great insight into the inner world of elite performance. It will help you in those key moments that define the difference between success and failure.'

Joe Choong MBE, Olympic champion, Tokyo 2020

'Charlie is at the forefront of performance psychology and his authentic approach is superb. He has helped me as a fighter pilot, as an advanced fast jet instructor and, more generally, in the way I live life.'

Group Captain Rob Caine MBE, RAF fighter pilot

'A ground-breaking philosophy for understanding and unlocking elite performance – essential reading for business leaders today.'

Tom Willis, CEO, Shoreham Port

'A wonderfully insightful and engaging book that can help us all meet the challenges we face and have some fun along the way.'

Owen Clay, Partner at Linklaters LLP

'Just superb. This book combines science with practical insight and tips to help all of us constantly improve while performing under pressure.'

Ed Williams QC, barrister

'Charlie says all the things which as a parent you want to say, but you just can't find the right words or the right time to say them.'

Parent

'Meet your secret weapon.'

Tatler *(extracted from a January 2019 feature on the author)*

Inside Out

Inside Out

*Train your mind and your nerve
like a champion*

CHARLIE UNWIN

NICHOLAS BREALEY
PUBLISHING
London • Boston

First published in Great Britain by Nicholas Brealey Publishing in 2022
An imprint of John Murray Press
A division of Hodder & Stoughton Ltd,
An Hachette UK company

1

Extracts on pp.17 and 20 from *What Sport Teaches Us about Life* by Ed Smith, published by
Penguin © 2008.
Extract on p. 50 from *The Stress Test* by Ian Robertson, published by
Bloomsbury Publishing © 2016.
Extracts on pp. 191 and 195 from *Flow* by Mihaly Csikszentmihalyi, published by
Harper & Row © 1990.

A CIP catalogue record for this title is available from the British Library

Hardback ISBN 978 1 529 36977 9
eBook ISBN 978 1 529 36980 9

Typeset by KnowledgeWorks Global Ltd.

Printed and bound in Great Britain by Clays Ltd, Elcograf S.p.A.

John Murray Press policy is to use papers that are natural, renewable and recyclable products
and made from wood grown in sustainable forests. The logging and manufacturing processes
are expected to conform to the environmental regulations of the country of origin.

John Murray Press	Nicholas Brealey Publishing
Carmelite House	Hachette Book Group
50 Victoria Embankment	Market Place, Center 53, State Street
London EC4Y 0DZ	Boston, MA 02109, USA

www.nicholasbrealey.com

Contents

Acknowledgements

I am so lucky to have had some amazing mentors on my journey through the military, sport and business. Thank you for asking the questions I was too scared to ask.

Thank you to my beautiful wife, Rose, without whom this book would not exist. You inspire me every day to be better and gift me the space to achieve it.

And finally to my mother, Jacqueline Unwin, who indulged me in my passions from the beginning and taught me life's most important lessons.

Introduction

Curiously, we only ever see ourselves on the outside, yet everything
happens on the inside.

The Cairo sun was blazing outside and making its presence felt inside.
Little effort had been made to air-condition the enormous hall, presumably to give the local athletes home advantage. Despite the heat,
my focus was squarely on the target stood 10 metres away. I had
completed 15 shots of a 20-shot pistol shooting competition, just
the beginning of a very long day. Still to come were three hours of
fencing, a 200-metre swim, a round of jumps, riding a horse that I
had never ridden before, and a 3-kilometre run. I had always dreamed
of being James Bond, but competing for my country in the sport of
modern pentathlon was the next best thing.

As I awaited the command, 'for your sixteenth shot, load', the
silence in the hall gave way to a disturbance at the back. A full-on brawl
had broken out between the Egyptian and Russian coaches, who had
clearly taken a dislike to each other. Menacing insults quickly turned
physical, and security had no option but to wade in and eject them
both from the hall. Despite their swift action, the damage had been
done and the orderly line of 30 athletes on the range had become
visibly agitated, pacing up and down along their firing positions and
sipping water from their drink bottles in an attempt to stay calm and
focused. It took at least 10 minutes for the competition to resume.

What happened next changed the course of my life.

On the command 'Load', I fed the pistol grip into my right hand
and took a deep breath as I loaded a pellet into the barrel of the gun.

Feeling a wave of relaxation run through my body, I raised the pistol onto the target, repeating the usual mantra in my head – 'Calm, control, sights'. As I squeezed the trigger and released the shot, I felt total focus, control and ease. The shot went straight through the centremost point of the target, known as the Centre Ten.

Over the course of the last five shots of the competition, the scores across the leaderboard dropped off a cliff. I can only imagine that Egyptian–Russian tensions had stolen the concentration of many of the athletes. Conversely, I achieved something I had never achieved before, not even in training. I shot five centre tens in a row and climbed from fifteenth position into the top three.

In itself, that wasn't enough to change my life (as great as it felt). It was more what happened immediately after. I packed up my pistol and walked to the back of the hall, where I was greeted by my coach. 'That was amazing,' he exclaimed. 'How did you manage to hold it together after that fight?'

I was confused by his question. 'What fight?' I genuinely had no recollection of there being a fight, or indeed that there had been any delay in the competition at all. At that point the Austrian coach approached me. He had noticed that, while all the other athletes had been walking around during the disruption, trying to stay calm and composed, I had remained rooted to the spot. Having observed my body language and eye movements he was convinced I was hypnotised!

At first I didn't know what to make of this information. Any of it. All I knew was that something had happened to me – it felt like a profound experience, different from anything else I had experienced before. And I had reason to believe that it wasn't a fluke – rather, it was thanks to a dramatic shift that I had made a year earlier in my approach to training.

It was around this time that I had been competing in another World Cup competition in Budapest. My experience could not have been more different. Under the pressure and expectation to get off to a good start, I remember feeling intense pulses of anxiety coupled with catastrophic thoughts of everything that could go wrong and what my coach would think of me if I didn't get the right result. It was my first ever World Cup and I remember thinking that I had to justify my selection on the team. It's amazing how many negative thoughts can race through your mind when they become untethered. Raising my arm to take the first shot, I literally had no control of the pistol. Shaking violently, I pulled the trigger and completely missed the target. It was 7.30am. I had 10 more hours of competition to go and already I was bottom of the pile. These are dangerous thoughts for an athlete – and, unsurprisingly, the day didn't get much better from there.

How could my experience of these two competitions have been so different when the situation I was in was almost identical?

After the disaster in Budapest I did a lot of soul-searching. I realised I had been making a huge assumption. An assumption that was unhelpful to me, an assumption that I now recognise most people make at some point in their quest to reach the top: 'The more I do in training, the better I will be in competition.'

This is certainly true up to a point, but then comes a brutal realisation that hours and hours of practice can count for nothing if at the all-important moment you present yourself tense and incoherent. And this can happen no matter how capable you are. It's easy to go through the motions of training and practice while failing to prepare ourselves for the psychological reality of doing it when it really counts.

Your inner world predicts your outer world

This is a book about personal leadership and high performance. It's about your ability to achieve incredible things on the outside by paying attention to what's on the inside.

So far in my career I've had the privilege to work with and learn from some of the very best in the world, from multiple Olympic champions to business leaders, Special Forces soldiers to global fashion designers, fighter pilots to international footballers. I have worked with them to develop the mental skills they need to perform consistently at their best, often under immense pressure. I am also eternally grateful that some of these people have agreed to share their amazing stories in this book. I know you will find them hugely insightful and inspiring.

There is something compelling about watching someone who is at the very top of their game, whether it's an athlete, a musician, a speaker, a surgeon, a comedian, a barrister, a soldier or a chef. A master of their craft has universal appeal, their skill is captivating and their passion is contagious. Naturally, we only get to see one dimension of their brilliance – the skills and behaviours we are able to physically observe. But the brilliance of their outer game hides the complex and dynamic interaction of forces that plays out beneath the surface. This matters. It's from here that everything ripples out. Our thoughts, our attention, our emotions, our breathing, our heart rate and our muscular tension all have leading roles in the drama that makes up our inner game, and they are all intrinsically connected. Therefore it goes without saying that true experts are marked by their capacity to undulate between the concrete external world (e.g. technical and physical) and their rather more abstract internal world (mental, emotional and intuitive).

At the heart of this Inside-Out philosophy is the idea that there is no real excellence in all this world that cannot be separated from the way we manage and conduct ourselves. Forget how the outside world looks in on you – the performance reviews, statistics and analysis – these things measure the impact you have had, but they tell you nothing of how it was achieved, or how it can be achieved again. Instead, you are at your most powerful when you focus on getting what you want out of the experience, the inner mastery that will lead to the impact you want on the outside.

In this book I want to share with you how the best in the world work on their inner performance, managing the thoughts, feelings and habits that allow them to relentlessly pursue and achieve excellence. More importantly, I want to share with you how this has shaped my approach to mental fitness and training, with the goal of helping you to apply the same principles to your own performance. Armed with plenty of practical examples and fascinating insights from some very different performance arenas, you will learn how elite athletes train their mind and body for peak performance, how Special Forces soldiers train for the intensity of high-stakes operations, how musicians find their flow, how City traders manage the emotions of a turbulent market, how extreme climbers expand their comfort zone and how 'Top Gun' fighter pilots develop unrivalled intuition.

INTRODUCTION

Training three dimensions: thinking, feeling and intuitive

If there's one thing we can say with total certainty about the achievements of high performers, it's that world records and gold medals don't happen by accident. My experience in Cairo reminds me of the potential we all have for our mind to guide our performance in extraordinary ways – but this requires us to have a clear strategy for how we train our focus, our confidence, our intuition, our emotional state, and our capacity to learn faster and deal with setbacks along the way.

For all my clients, good psychology is not simply about how they react to challenging events, it is also about how they condition their mind and physiology day in, day out. This is something we now understand much better thanks to the rapid advances in neuropsychology and biofeedback which inform my Inside-Out approach. For me, this has shifted the emphasis from giving people 'coping strategies' for surviving setbacks and dealing with important events towards an approach which emphasises day-to-day training of mental fitness. This is a far more proactive approach that places positive psychology at the heart of everything we do.

With this in mind, my Inside-Out approach consists of three dimensions of inner performance which form the three parts of this book:

- The Thinking Dimension
- The Feeling Dimension
- The Intuitive Dimension.

The Thinking Dimension

The Thinking Dimension is responsible for delivering focus to your performance. In the same way that you might measure a computer by its processing power, the Thinking Dimension boils down to your ability to think clearly and effectively. The Thinking Dimension is managed largely by the frontal lobes of the brain. Referred to as the 'rational' brain, the frontal lobes are responsible for helping us to apply logic and intelligence to challenging situations. In doing so, they control higher-order functions such as planning, problem solving and anticipation as well as giving you a sense of time and context.

High performance relies heavily on these core functions. With experience and expertise you can develop your own neural 'architecture', which allows you to refine the way you think and focus over time. Mental training is about being proactive in this process, accelerating the pathways of success.

You are at your best in this dimension when you are thinking clearly and positively. You make confident, timely decisions that inform the quality and precision of your actions. You have a consistent and positive mindset that helps you to stay focused on what you can control while accepting what you can't. This is both a process and a philosophy which become part of your everyday mindset. This mindset informs the way you invite challenge, respond to praise and criticism, and deal with success and failure. You are also at your best in this dimension when you are actively learning. You will be able to absorb more from every experience, thereby accelerating your rate of improvement.

The Feeling Dimension

The Feeling Dimension is ultimately responsible for delivering and managing energy. The Feeling Dimension is governed by physiological activity in the nervous system and, in particular, your stress response. This is overseen by the brain's limbic system, otherwise referred to as the 'emotional' brain. This is a complex collection of structures in the core of the brain which receive sensory information from all around the body. These signals arrive up through the brain stem and into the limbic system. Like a highly sophisticated smoke alarm, the limbic system constantly monitors for threat and is the judge of what is pleasurable or scary. It also determines how our body reacts. Whenever there is something to win or lose, it activates the body's stress response – releasing energy to our brain and muscles. This reaction happens in the blink of an eye and without conscious control, making feelings of excitement, nervousness and anticipation an inevitable part of the human experience. But that's not to say we can't teach our body to respond differently to stress over time. We can also choose to interpret these feelings differently (e.g. 'I feel excited' rather than 'I feel scared'), a skill which often separates those who are rooted to the spot in fear from those who seem to perform with effortless freedom.

In the Feeling Dimension I'm going to be showing you how to proactively train your response to stress and the emotions of high-pressure environments. I will also share some great techniques for using controlled exposure to stress as a way of strengthening your nerve.

For the purposes of structuring a clear approach to mental training, it's much easier to separate the Thinking Dimension and the Feeling Dimension and focus on them separately. But in reality they are intrinsically linked – focus and energy need each other. If you have focus but no energy, then you will lack urgency, perseverance and creativity. If you have energy but no focus, you will lack direction, productivity and learning.

The Intuitive Dimension

The Intuitive Dimension is responsible for mobilising all your past experience into one moment, allowing you to think without thinking. This is your highly skilled and proficient autopilot. Whereas the Thinking and Feeling Dimensions can be accessed consciously, the Intuitive Dimension harnesses the incredible power of your subconscious.

The Intuitive Dimension is all about your brain's ability to match patterns, something it can do better and faster than any supercomputer known to man. This allows you to perceive a situation with the collective wisdom of all your senses and all your past experiences coming together, creating what some might call your sixth sense.

For reasons we will discover, this is arguably the most powerful tool in your amoury, if harnessed correctly. We all have this sixth sense and we are all dependent on it to live and operate effectively. However, we often don't make the most of it because we either don't develop it properly in the first place or we smother it by not listening to it.

Our Intuitive Dimension is somewhat mysterious since you cannot measure or control it directly, but you can develop your 'intuitive library' – the database of experience that your intuition uses. Many of the professionals I have worked with in this book owe their success to the steps they have taken to nurture, educate and shape their intuitive responses to everyday challenges. They have often formed mental processes and habits so effective that they are completely unaware of themselves responding to critical moments. It's so natural to them you'd be forgiven for thinking it's part of their DNA, when actually it's been honed over many years, slowly influencing every other part of the performance system from the Inside Out.

By using these three dimensions to maximise the wealth of resources you have on the inside, you may be surprised by the impact you are capable of having on the outside. I would like the Inside Out mindset to help you to understand your inner potential and to build confidence in your ability to invite challenge and thrive. Many of the professionals I work with apply themselves to mental training because it's an essential part of achieving their goals. It's not because they are special or set apart from anyone else. Yet so many times I have heard self-labelled 'amateurs' convincing themselves that mental training is the preserve of the top professionals. In my opinion, this couldn't be further from the truth. For most people it's not about being the best in the world; it's simply about putting your best foot forward no matter what your goal in life is. It's about having the impact you want to have and expressing the best version of yourself in everyday situations – from the Inside Out.

PART I

The Thinking Dimension

'Experience is not what happens to a man; it is what a man does with what happens to him.'

Aldous Huxley

Be the architect of your own mind

There's no more terrifying way to travel down a mountain than on a skeleton sled. You're sliding down an ice run lying headfirst on your stomach, reaching speeds of up to 90mph, your chin just centimetres above the track. You're steering the sled with subtle movements of your head and shoulders, looking for a precise line into the next curve which sweeps up above you. As you go round the corner, the force of gravity presses down on your body to a peak of 6G. That's comparable to the pressure experienced by Formula 1 drivers, fighter pilots and astronauts at take-off, but you're much more exposed. All that lies between you and the ice is a narrow sled and a thin skin of Lycra. One tiny mistake and your body smashes into the ice, making it almost impossible to regain control. And even if you don't wipe out or pinball down the track, athletes can get nose bleeds and have been known to pass out halfway down the mountain.

In 2012 I was given the privileged opportunity to work with Great Britain's Winter Olympic Skeleton Team as their mental coach. I was gripped by the sport from day one, with the psychological dynamics giving me plenty to work with. Introduced to a small bunch of ambitious but relatively inexperienced athletes, little did I realise what they would go on to achieve. Following on from the success of Amy Williams, who landed Britain's first ever gold medal in the sport at the 2010 Games in Vancouver, Lizzy Yarnold went on to surpass this by becoming the first ever double Winter Olympic champion, with success in Sochi in 2014 and Pyeongchang in 2018. With Lizzy's teammates Dominic Parsons and Laura Deas each winning a bronze medal in Pyeongchang, this small bunch of overachievers became Britain's most successful team in Winter Olympic history.

On the face of it, Great Britain had no right to be so successful in this sport. There isn't a single skeleton track in Britain, and compared with the bigger Winter Olympic nations like the United States, Canada, Russia, Germany and France, Britain has never had a culture of winter sports, let alone the knowledge, the resources and the opportunities for the athletes to practise.

It's my belief that Britain became the number one skeleton nation in the world not in spite of these challenges but because of them. If we had copied the bigger nations, we would only ever have been second-rate versions of them. Instead we had the opportunity to start with a blank sheet of paper and ask one simple question: 'What gets us from the top of the mountain to the bottom as quickly as possible?'

For a team that starts from a position of established success, innovation feels risky and threatening. For a team that starts with a blank sheet of paper, innovation feels progressive, even exhilarating. It was a joy to work with some great sport scientists along the way, all of whom became experts at applying their knowledge to novel situations. It was no different in the psychology department where we asked the British sliders to experiment and innovate with their mental game. If they were going to win medals, they were going to have to think differently from their international rivals.

As Great Britain's most successful Winter Olympic athlete of all time, there were many things that contributed towards Lizzy Yarnold's exceptional record, but one of those was undoubtedly the way she processed information and organised her mind. As with most professions, there is enough uncertainty in the world around us without creating our own uncertainty within. Therefore success in the Thinking Dimension is all about establishing confidence and consistency in your own mind, to think correctly and to stay focused in otherwise complex and ambiguous situations. To achieve this we will need to address two key components – mental *attitude* and mental *aptitude*.

In the first half of the Thinking Dimension we will explore mental *attitude*. This refers to the mindset you adopt in critical situations. By learning how to adapt this mindset, you can achieve very different results. I've always imagined our mindset as the mental gatekeeper and guardian of what we allow in and what we keep out. Our mindset becomes an unconscious filter for what we pay attention to and the way we make sense of the world around us. If this filter is working well for us, it enables us to pay attention to the things that enrich our experience and help us in our endeavours. As a result, we tend to enjoy greater clarity and insight, we seek opportunities to learn and get better, and we feel greater satisfaction and fulfilment. This relates to a specific mode of activity in the brain that neuroscientists call the 'reward-approach' mode.

The alternative to this is the 'threat-avoidance' mode, where we find ourselves paying attention to the things that threaten us and stand in our way. We start to behave in a manner that limits our potential – often without realising it. As we will discover, shaping your mindset is an important first step in training the Thinking Dimension.

In the second half of the Thinking Dimension we focus on mental *aptitude*. This is all about applying yourself intelligently to the goals you set. We explore how you can enhance your everyday experience by being more mindful of the lessons presented to you, thereby accelerating the rate at which you are capable of learning and adapting. Many people think of learning as a discrete activity which happens while in a classroom, reading a book or following an online programme. But from a neurological standpoint, learning is about making, refining and strengthening connections in the brain, a process that is happening all the time in response to the world around us. By being active rather than passive in this process, elite performers are able to enhance their capacity to think clearly and apply themselves to new and novel situations.

Section 1: Mental attitude: the Inside-Out mindset

'The moment of victory is far too short for a person to live for that and nothing else.'

Martina Navratilova

I

Attitude: changing the way you think about success

In the world of high performance, your attitude is essential. Experience and skill mean nothing if you are constantly sabotaging your own efforts from within.

For this reason, 'mindset' often gets cited as a fundamental selection criterion within the talent programmes of many organisations, as well as for new recruits and employees. The assumption here is that your attitude to learning and self-improvement is a better predictor of future success than your current knowledge, skill or ability. The problem here is that mindset is notoriously difficult to measure!

In my experience mindset is best observed when a) people are being challenged to the edge of their ability and b) there is something to win or lose.

The beauty of a sport like skeleton is that you can send recruits down an ice track in a relatively safe manner from the outset. It's not pretty to watch, but through careful observation you can answer the following questions:

- What is their ability to analyse and solve problems in a logical way?
- What is their ability to make clear decisions and stay committed to a course of action?
- Who is brave enough to actually do the right thing?
- What is their attitude to learning and getting better?
- How do they respond to failure?
- How do they respond to success?
- How do they respond to the success of other people around them?
- How do they respond to feedback?
- How well do they do all of the above under pressure?

So why are these questions so important, and what do they say about our capacity to make the most of what we have? For many of the clients I work with, their initial motivation for engaging with psychology is often born out of frustration. They feel frustrated at not being able to consistently get the results they know they are capable of. It's almost like they are getting in their own way, tripping themselves up.

There is a multitude of reasons for this, such as over-competitiveness, fear of other people's opinions, poor self-awareness, lack of confidence, or lack of willingness to challenge themselves or to move to the next level. Other reasons could include difficulty in taking feedback or criticism, or, having been successful before, a struggle to get back to high performance, including the challenges of returning from injury for athletes. Other people feel as though they should be further ahead than they are, or are unable to experience pride or satisfaction and are struggling with seeing others make more progress than them, or are dealing with other people's expectations ... The list goes on.

All of these mental trip hazards have a way of inhibiting your ability to perform with freedom. You either end up trying too hard, or you become disengaged from the challenge at hand – a passenger on your own ride. Aware of what you should be doing, you can't seem to do it – your thoughts, communication, even your movement become stunted and incoherent.

These are common ailments in many working environments, but especially in high-pressure industries. They represent a very human struggle. But chances are you didn't think like this when you started out on your chosen path. In the beginning, you probably never thought about your opponents because they didn't seem to have much relevance to your own initial progression. You never worried about making mistakes because they were just par for the course – part of the 'have a go' mentality. You never cared about what anyone else thought because you had no reputation to protect. You had never planned for these thoughts to suddenly arrive one day and trip you up – just as things were starting to get serious.

After hundreds, possibly thousands, of personal conversations getting underneath the surface of some of these internal interferences,

I realised that the world's top performers still have these thoughts. You always imagine they are free from the scourge of insecurity and negative thinking, but I can assure you they are not. Some are afflicted by perfectionism and competitiveness, yet it doesn't seem to undermine their ability to perform in the same way it does for others. How can that be? The answer to that lies within the ancient proverb: we all have a good dragon and we all have a bad dragon; the one that wins is the one you feed the most.

This principle is the epicentre of positive psychology. It is guided by an important truism about how our brains work. If I tell you *not* to think of a yellow car, you will probably start thinking of a yellow car. The more I urge you not to think of a yellow car, the more it reinforces the image of a yellow car in your mind. If I now incentivise you to not think of a yellow car by offering you a substantial cash reward which you can have only if you keep it from your mind for two minutes, do you think this incentive will help you or hinder you?

So how do you not think of a yellow car? Think of a blue car maybe? But don't just think of any blue car, think of a dark metallic blue car. Imagine every detail of it, from the alloy wheels to the silver trim around its tinted windows. In fact, the more detail you go into with the blue car, the more compelling the image becomes. It holds your attention. This is exactly how your brain works, where every thought equates to the activation of a neural pathway. The more that thought is practised, the easier it becomes for that pathway to fire. You cannot 'undo' a physical pathway in the brain. You can only encourage the energy to be redirected down a more helpful pathway. Very often the reason we find ourselves having unhelpful negative thoughts isn't because we are negative people, it's because we haven't truly invested in a positive alternative, a clear image of what good looks like.

This is a common challenge within many work environments. Managers think they are incentivising their teams to perform better, when what they are really communicating is: 'Don't perform badly.' Why? Because poor performance is often defined and spoken about far more than good performance. If you are performing well, you largely get ignored, but those performing badly get regular attention from their leaders until they have developed a highly sophisticated and nuanced language for poor performance and underachievement. They become acutely aware of every mistake to avoid at every point in the process. Working life becomes a series of trip hazards and success is defined by the ability to avoid them. This makes a culture of underperformance remarkably easy to attain.

In essence, what I have discovered is that top performers are not immune to negative thoughts. The difference is they have invested a great deal of mental energy in imagining and reimagining what good looks and feels like, so the negative thoughts never really get a chance to grow. This may be something they have created for themselves, or it may be something they have had help with from some great coaches and mentors around them. Either way, we can all get better at shaping our mindset.

Positive psychology goes further than this. Where you place your attention and invest your thoughts is intrinsically connected to how you feel. If you are good at managing your attention, you can also manage your mood and energy. Conversely, when your mood and energy are lifted, you are more likely to embrace challenge and relax into it, interpret your environment favourably, and adopt a more positive belief about yourself; even your memory and intuition improve. By expecting and imagining a positive experience, you are more likely to get one.

Where your attention goes, your body follows, so let's now get beneath the surface of your mindset, looking at how to understand it and, most importantly, how to train it.

The advantage of being a beginner or underdog

One of the great privileges of my job is learning about the stories of amazing people, teams and organisations that have achieved incredible things. One narrative that persistently appears in these conversations is the struggle they've been through to get where they are today. Inevitably, things haven't been handed to them on a plate. This narrative often starts from a young age and has a profound effect on the way their mentality is shaped and therefore how they face future challenges.

My early research in sport led me to a fascinating phenomenon called younger sibling syndrome. YSS neatly explains why so many highly successful individuals reference their playground rivalry with older siblings as being key to shaping them. Serena Williams, Andy Murray and Michael Jordan are just some of the athletes who have benefited from being younger siblings. Professor Mark Williams at the University of Utah found that, across 33 sports, younger siblings were significantly more likely to outperform their older siblings at the highest level.[1] A 2010 study by Frank Sulloway and Richard Zweigenhaft of 700 pairs of brothers who played in Major League Baseball found that younger brothers were two and a half times more likely than their older brothers to record superior career batting statistics. Overall, among hitters and pitchers, younger brothers also played an average of two and a half years longer than older brothers.[2]

To help explain YSS, I'll draw upon my own humble experience playing cricket in the garden with my older brother when we were kids. It probably won't be a surprise to readers that I am the younger brother, which is why I love telling this story, and equally why my brother hates hearing it.

Being older than me, Benjie was always one step ahead in his development – he was bigger, stronger, faster and more coordinated. Basically, I had no chance of beating him. Without being consciously aware of it, my motivation for playing was shaped more by my intrinsic enjoyment of practising and getting better at little elements of the game rather than worrying about the eventual outcome.

I remember one day having the bat in my hand and somehow managing to connect sweetly with the ball that my brother had pelted towards me. Maybe more by luck than design, the ball went flying across the garden and landed in a bush at the far end. As Benjie went off to look for it I was left for a moment with time to reflect. How did I do that? I came to two conclusions. One was that I kept focusing on the ball all the way onto the bat; the other was I kept my bat straight so it had a greater chance of connecting with the ball. I later learned that these were two very good tips for cricketers.

From that point onwards, I focused as though my life depended on it, keeping my eye on the ball and keeping a straight bat. It became my focus and my motivation rolled into one. I still couldn't beat Benjie, but I *could* get better at these two skills if I applied myself. For a while at least, these two things became my reason for wanting to play, and this was further reinforced by the fact that the more I worked at them, the more I could see myself progressing. I was hitting the ball more consistently, which then meant I was scoring more points. This is what I call an Inside-Out mindset, where the primary focus and motivation are centred on the process that delivers results, rather than on the results themselves.

After a lot of hard work, the day eventually came when I managed to beat Benjie. My process had become good enough to match my brother's ability. And that was the day my brother folded his arms in despair and said, 'I don't want to play this anymore.' And that was that. I'm not sure we've played since.

Of course, the challenge for him was that winning had been relatively easy up until that point. He hadn't needed to apply the same amount of focus and energy to his game as I had had to, which meant that, when the outcome didn't go to plan, his motivation (and no doubt his ego) took a tumble, with little to fall back on. This is the point when our pursuit of success becomes a threat rather than an opportunity, the point that exposes the vulnerabilities of an Outside-In mindset. This is where we are so preoccupied with the outcome that it dilutes and disrupts our ability to pay attention to the process and skills for achieving it.

Now, before all you older siblings hurl this book across the room at your little brothers and sisters in disgust (if you haven't already), rest assured you are not doomed to be second rate in all your endeavours – there are still plenty of very successful older siblings out there. That's because it's not actually being a younger sibling that's important here. What's important is the mindset they have been encouraged to adopt. In fact, you could just as easily call it the beginner's effect.

As beginners at any activity, we are able to tune back into our childhood ability to learn without hindrance. Children are masters at learning – it's their superpower. They're inquisitive, keen to have a go, and they fail so much in their quest to get better at something that failing really doesn't faze them. I'm not sure they would even consider that they've failed – failure is more of an adult concept. Instead, something hasn't happened as they wanted it to happen and they are curious as to how they can change it.

This is the starting point of any journey towards excellence. It also happens to be the point at which we tend to be most open to new ideas and skills – we are doing it for fun, we are doing it with a sense of freedom and play, and progress is easy. A beginner really does have the most powerful mindset towards their chosen specialism. But maintaining this mindset for learning and mastery when we have experienced the sweet nectar of success and when we start to place expectation on future outcomes, that is the true measure of a champion.

As always, it's easy to commentate on the people who do this well, putting them on a pedestal, but the truth is that, once we understand this principle, we can all get better at nurturing an Inside-Out mindset. To help us formalise this into something we can actually develop for ourselves, I would like to share my approach with you.

Defining success

I have noticed there are three universal ways that people define success: mastery, metrics and outcome.

1 **Mastery** This represents everything you can control and improve. It is an internal measure of success, focusing on the continuous development of key skills, specific techniques and routines that advance you towards your goals. Some of these skills you might really enjoy; others you know you have to do and get better at if you want to move closer to your ultimate goals. In the garden with my brother my mastery goals were keeping my eye on the ball and keeping a straight bat.

2 **Metrics** This is a way of measuring your progress towards your outcome but it's not the outcome itself – rather, it is a proxy. Many industries call these key performance indicators (KPIs). In the garden with my brother my KPIs were clean hits of the ball and scoring runs (points).

3 **Outcome** This is an external measure of success – it's about achieving results as defined by the outside world. The outcome is about mission success, whatever your mission is – winning, status, power, reputation, financial success, etc. An athlete might dream of winning gold, a lawyer might dream of becoming a partner at their firm. In the garden playing cricket the ultimate outcome was to win against my brother.

Figures 1.1 and 1.2 highlight the difference between an Inside-Out mindset and an Outside-In mindset. With an Inside-Out mindset (Figure 1.1) you stay focused on the core skills, techniques and processes for achieving a successful outcome. In doing so, you will stay focused on the controllable present, paying attention to the quality of your input and being curious as to what you could do better. These are the things you can ultimately control in any situation.

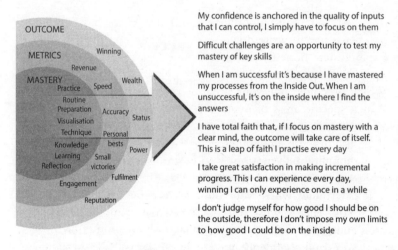

My confidence is anchored in the quality of inputs that I can control, I simply have to focus on them

Difficult challenges are an opportunity to test my mastery of key skills

When I am successful it's because I have mastered my processes from the Inside Out. When I am unsuccessful, it's on the inside where I find the answers

I have total faith that, if I focus on mastery with a clear mind, the outcome will take care of itself. This is a leap of faith I practise every day

I take great satisfaction in making incremental progress. This I can experience every day, winning I can only experience once in a while

I don't judge myself for how good I should be on the outside, therefore I don't impose my own limits to how good I could be on the inside

FIGURE 1.1 Illustration of an Inside-Out mindset

In contrast, Figure 1.2 illustrates an Outside-In mindset. This is where you become fixated on the future outcome and results of what you are doing. Here it is easy to start comparing yourself with other people while becoming preoccupied with how you 'should' be doing. This creates unhelpful judgement and distraction at the very point you need to focus on the quality of your game.

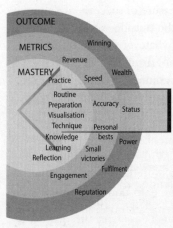

I am so invested in the outcome that I struggle to focus on the details and smaller steps to getting there

The more pressure I am under, the more I am scared of failing

I care more about how I am doing and what other people think of me than I do about my own process for achieving my goals

I often feel like a passenger in the environment I am in, aware of what's happening but unable to do much about it. This makes me feel vulnerable

Other competitors are a threat to my success, therefore I focus more on them than I do myself

If I am successful, I feel relief; if I am unsuccessful, I feel dismay and unclear what to do. I rarely feel pride or genuine satisfaction

I don't take many risks for fear of failure. Therefore I am probably not demonstrating my true potential

FIGURE 1.2 Illustration of an Outside–In mindset

The first and most important step in developing an Inside–Out mindset is just to write down your mastery, metrics and outcomes. Explore them honestly and think about their relationship with one another. Which ones are particularly helpful or unhelpful to you? Which outcomes pull your attention away from mastery the most? Which specific areas of mastery do you enjoy practising the most and which are more of a discipline? It's my observation that your awareness of these three different types of goals and how they affect your thoughts and emotions is often the most influential factor in achieving your potential – and I don't say that lightly.

It determines where your thoughts and feelings go, where you invest your energy, what you feel threatened by, and therefore how stress and anxiety affect you. It determines the consistency of your motivation and confidence, your ability to overcome obstacles, your willingness to take feedback, and your ability to experience pride, satisfaction and, ultimately, fulfilment.

Some industries are better than others at differentiating performance (inputs) from results (outputs). Only when you understand the difference can you guide your attention proactively. A swimmer wanting to break the world record isn't thinking about the world record during the race; they are thinking about the quality of their dive, the length of their stroke and the speed of their turns. Get these inputs right and they give themselves the best chance of breaking the record.

Sprinter Usain Bolt is a fascinating example of this principle. Up to the age of 15 he was never shown his times in training. As a youngster it was clear he had amazing potential, but his coach and mentor, Pablo McNeil, described the young Usain as being easily distracted by external adoration, leaving the school grounds to take a taxi and flirt with girls – he was a typical teenager, right? When it came to his sport, Usain was starting to attract huge attention, not least from the Jamaican prime minister, who addressed him as an 'outstanding talent'. It was Pablo's job to maximise this potential, and in doing so he knew he needed to keep Usain focused on the quality and enjoyment of his training, not on the measures that set him apart from other people. Even in the latter stages of his sprinting career you could see the energy and enjoyment he brought to daily training – every session was fun, but there was intent and hard work.

At this point I should make a really important point. Do not confuse the idea of not focusing on the outcome with not caring about the outcome. If you didn't care about the outcome, you would never have the motivation to want to get better in the first place. The greatest performers I've ever worked with have all shared a deep desire to achieve success and they take competitiveness to another level. But fundamentally they channel this energy into understanding what makes them good, investing in the quality of everyday processes, such that they always focus on their own performance, often with little regard for anyone else's unless they can learn something from it. They may care deeply about the output, but they invest their study and attention on the input.

This is one of the great paradoxes of high performance. In order to achieve the best results that you are capable of, you must focus on the mastery of what you do. It is this that allows you to stay connected with the moment you are in and the process that guides you. The second you start ruminating on the consequences of winning or losing, you entertain a future that is at least one step removed from your control. This induces a threat response (the brain hates what can't be controlled or predicted), which in turn pulls your attention away from your guiding focus. The greater the consequences of success and failure, the greater the pull, and the more confidence you must have in your base skills – performing from the Inside Out.

Doing it for the love of it

I often think about the final training session of David Beckham's career. It was the eve of his last appearance for Paris Saint-Germain and he stayed behind to practise his free kicks, long after his team-mates had left. Even then, after everything he had accomplished with Manchester United, Real Madrid, Milan and England, and all the goals he had scored from free kicks, Beckham was still trying to get better. This is a poignant image, and the archetypal example of an Inside-Out mindset that demonstrates the power of doing something for the sheer love of it.

We've all been there at some point in our lives – you get *good enough* to achieve a predetermined level of success; then you stop applying the same conscious effort to getting better. But is it the same kind of effort for someone who truly loves what they do?

As you embark upon a new endeavour with a puppyish enthusiasm, you get to a point where further progression requires far more consideration. Effort becomes code for discipline, sacrifice and, sometimes, reluctance. Yet you would never expect a child to put 'effort' into playing – that makes no sense. They play because they want to and would do so all day if they could.

The difference is that we don't impose an end goal on a child's play – they still have intentions that keep them focused on mini-goals and make their play progressive – but ultimately they are doing it for the intrinsic love of being in that moment and therefore they are free from any of the psychological shackles that we as adults seem to place on ourselves. This state of 'doing it for the sheer love of doing it' is called a 'self-determined' state, and it's immensely powerful. The more self-determined you are, the more persistent you are in the face of obstacles, the more discretionary effort you apply and the more vitality you have. You are more likely to interpret stress as positive energy, making it eustress (short for euphoric stress), rather than distress. We talk more about these two types of stress in the Feeling Dimension.

No wonder self-determination is considered the holy grail by the progressive industries of Silicon Valley, some of which invest huge amounts of money in better understanding this priceless ingredient of human psychology. Away from Silicon Valley, it's a state that companies like Dyson try to tap into by giving their engineers the freedom and space to innovate – to operate in the open mode of creativity, intuition and possibility, rather than the closed mode of expectation, results and deadlines.

When Inside Out turns to Outside In

What causes us to shift from an Inside-Out mindset, where our attention and energy are anchored by the mastery and intrinsic love of what we do, to an Outside-In mindset, where our attention edges towards results, reputation and expectation?

All ambitious individuals have to battle their fears and anxieties at some point – it's simply part of the performance equation. When you have a vision for yourself, you become invested in that image – every time you think about where you want to get to, you colour in this image a bit more. In doing so, you must be prepared to accommodate the ebbs and flows of emotions that emerge from it. Feeling excited and satisfied when you make tangible steps towards your vision. Feeling guilt and fear when you fall below the curve you expect yourself to be on. It's these emotions that keep you going and keep you true to your goal.

I was incredibly lucky as a full-time athlete to be supported by the British Army with whom I served as an officer. The army couldn't have been more accommodating, but always hanging above me was the need to justify their faith in me. I later came to realise the extent to which other managers, leaders and athletes feel the same. For some, the threat is all too real – if you don't perform, you will be gone.

This is the consequence for a football manager who loses their first few games, a medical student who fails their final exams, a salesperson who doesn't sell enough, an SAS soldier who fails to maintain their combat skills, a partner at a law firm who fails to attract enough new business. High performers live on the brink of disappointment and failure, and with it the fear of having to retreat back into 'normal' life with their dreams unfulfilled. Depending on your mindset, this can either give you the kick up the bum you need or it can further your mental fragility and downward spiral, causing your form to worsen still further. Despite this, there should only ever be one thing that really matters – doing a good job.

This sounds obvious, doesn't it? But it's amazing how easy it is to be seduced by the pitfalls of money, politics, expectation and false adoration in favour of the core skills that made us successful in the first place. As Ed Smith, a former England cricketer and now the England national selector, said:

> Don't let anything come between you and playing well. Remove the obstacle to playing well… Thinking too far ahead of yourself is one of the obstacles. Not playing in the now is one of the obstacles. Failing to focus only and simply on the job in hand is one of the obstacles. Believing your life and your struggle to be disproportionately important is one of the obstacles. Dreading failure is one of the obstacles.[3]

It's easy to see how this steadfast focus on learning and mastery that you once enjoyed as a beginner slowly gets eroded from the Outside In by the need for results. This shift from an Inside-Out to an Outside-In mindset is often a subtle one, which happens slowly over time. It's common to see people who have excelled on their journey to the top, only to then lose their intensity of learning and their intrinsic passion for the minutiae of what they do. They genuinely believe they are applying the same effort as they always did, but in reality the intensity and connection with what they do have been lost and they are merely going through the motions.

The true measure of a champion is not simply someone who demonstrates an Inside-Out mindset (this is a gift we all start out with). It's someone who maintains this mindset no matter how successful and famous they become.

2

Talent: a blessing or a curse?

One of the most powerful studies to demonstrate how easily our mindset can shift was conducted by Professor Carol Dweck at Stanford University. Dweck and her researchers took 400 fifth-grade students and gave them a simple IQ task. On completion, one group was given the feedback: 'You did brilliantly, you must be really smart at this.' The other group were told: 'You did brilliantly, you must have worked really hard at this.'[1] This sounds like a very subtle difference in feedback, but the impact it had was frightening.

In phase two of the study, the same students were asked to complete another task, but this time they were able to choose whether they did a harder task or an easier task. Of the group who were praised for their intelligence, 67 per cent decided to have a go at the harder task. But of the group praised for their effort, an incredible 92 per cent went for the hard task.

The study didn't stop there. Having completed the second task, the students were told to write a note to their parents telling them how they did. Of the group originally given praise for their intelligence, a whopping 44 per cent lied about their results. Of the group originally praised for the effort they put in (most of whom chose the harder task), only 4 per cent lied about how they had got on.

How can one seemingly innocuous shift in the feedback these students received possibly take them down such a different path? Those children and adults praised for being smart are likely to assume that they are valued most for their intelligence. Therefore they avoid anything that might disprove this evaluation. As a result they play it safe and limit their potential for growth and improvement. There is a danger that their performance becomes driven by threat rather than by reward. For children and adults valued for their effort, including the way they stretch themselves and the quality of their practice, the result is that they don't worry that if they make a mistake people will think they are not talented; instead they think, 'If I don't take on hard things and stick to them, I'm not going to get better.'

This study highlights the sad reality for many kids who are labelled as 'talented' from a young age. Talent has a nasty knack of protecting the talented from the urge to self-improve. Never having needed resilience thus far, they fail to develop the mental and emotional versatility required at the top level. Before long they put more effort into managing their reputation for fear of losing it than they do into learning new skills and nurturing the quality of what they do.

I think that if you took a sample of any top team across any industry, you would find relatively few of the school prodigies who were destined to go all the way. Instead, you would find more of those kids who learned how to front up to another day of being judged and measured, bouncing back from disappointment and navigating tricky obstacles. As Ed Smith observed, 'The late developers, stubborn survivors and consistent over-performers have elbowed aside quite a few of the predestined stars.'

Confusing talent with potential

Just as our perception of talent can be overplayed, our perception of *potential* can be underplayed. Traditionally, these two have been perceived as the same thing – 'that kid is exceptional therefore they have huge potential'. As we've already seen with younger sibling syndrome, this is simply not the case. Just because they stand out at the age of 12 doesn't mean they will stand out further down the line. Likewise, seemingly average young performers have gone on to become the best in the world.

When footballer Lionel Messi was 12, he was having to endure growth hormone injections into his legs every day for a deficiency (GHD) that stopped him from developing properly. Messi was told repeatedly as a youngster that he was too small to play football professionally, let alone win FIFA World Player of the Year alongside four Champions League titles and six coveted Ballons d'Or (as he went on to do).

Potential is not a measure of where you are right now; rather it's about your capacity to improve. Naturally, this is far harder to measure, but some of the best teams and organisations are starting to do just that, and it requires them to understand what's on the inside, not on the outside.

In 2017 English football's Premier League invited a group of professional mentors from other sports and industries to work with their coaches. I was fortunate enough to be one of them. Their ultimate goal was to develop and transition more home-grown talent into top-flight football, thereby also benefiting the national team further down the line. The identification and development of talent had been something that UK nations had excelled at in Olympic sport, with Great Britain (a relative minnow) finishing second in the Rio Olympic Games medals table just a year earlier.

Up to that point I had always assumed that with the millions of pounds invested in Premier League academies, home-grown talent would be well represented, but how wrong I had been. At that point in time approximately 1 in 2,000 players from youth academies were getting professional contracts with Premier League clubs.

This suggests one of two things. Either there was an appalling lack of talent available in the UK when it comes to football (difficult to believe). Or there was little appetite for developing potential – instead it was easier to pay an extortionate amount of money for foreign talent with a proven record. It seemed a lot easier and safer to do this. In doing so, clubs were overvaluing 'talent' and undervaluing 'potential', and when this is their only strategy, it has a number of negative consequences. It relies heavily on having the financial resources to back it up, which adds to the pressure placed on management. It also creates a greater divide between 'star' players and the rest (which is linked to a player's intrinsic sense of value and self-confidence). In addition, clubs start to undermine the potential of their own academies, which work hard in the background to develop young players from as early as seven years old.

Our role within the Premier League's Coach Development Programme was not only to help the coaches in this quest but also to make the case for being braver and more confident at getting *potential* recognised over *talent*. This is made easier when principles such as mindset become a shared language among coaches. For example, coaches were becoming more skilled at looking beyond the immediate success or failure of any task and instead picking up on how the young players were responding to challenging situations. They started to engage players with the underlying principles of the training session rather than just getting them to 'do as they were told'. They got players thinking well beyond their next game at the weekend, and they helped players to overcome their competitive biases in order to learn from each other, even if they were competing for the same spot.

Importantly, this significant shift in attitude towards young players was being echoed by the national team and spearheaded by Gareth Southgate. One example of this was the development of a national centre for the England team at St George's Park in rural Staffordshire. The vision of the centre was to bring coaches, players and staff of all age groups, men and women, together under one roof. This would create a unified identity (much like Team GB was designed to unify 27 otherwise disparate Olympic sports) as well as a sense of continuity across the age groups as young players developed into senior players. It would also provide an environment where positive values and commitment to excellence could be expressed, and a secure base where players and staff could feel at home.

Such a huge change within an establishment requires enough brave people to think differently. It sounds like a no-brainer in hindsight, but resistance to the venture was significant and the project was initially rejected. Luckily, Gareth, with a supportive team around him, didn't give up. St George's Park was eventually built and opened in 2012 along with a 10-year plan for developing the talent that they hoped would fill it. The centre now provides facilities and headquarters for national teams from the age of 14 upwards, including 12 world-class pitches and a life-size replica of the Wembley pitch. It also has state-of-the-art hydrotherapy suites, biomechanics and training gyms, video analysis amenities, educational and coaching suites, and medical and sport science facilities.

I remember arriving at St George's for the first time when I had the opportunity to work with players and coaches prior to the 2016 World Cup. The architecture of the main entrance building matched the experience of working there – welcoming and inspiring.

It's a wonderful example of a 'psychologically informed environment' where great effort is taken to create an atmosphere that matches the intent. The motivational quotes and images around the training facilities inspire total commitment to every activity as well as a sense of 'teamness' and belonging. In contrast, the bedrooms are a safe space for maximising recovery and relaxation, decked out with familiar home comforts and pictures of family.

England manager Gareth Southgate's forward-thinking approach to developing young talent started to pay dividends well before the completion of his initial 10-year plan. In 2017, after just five years, the England Under-20 and Under-17 teams both won the FIFA World Cup and the Under-19 team won the UEFA European Cup. A few years later, England's senior team started to enjoy its best results for 50 years at major championships. This joined-up effort is also paying dividends at club level, with a 50 per cent increase in 'home-grown' players signing senior contracts with Premier League clubs in the five years up to 2021.

The temptation to focus on 'talent' over 'potential' is prevalent in many performance arenas, not least the selection of Special Forces soldiers. The lengthy and robust selection process for identifying those who will fare best in the Special Air Service (SAS) and the Special Boat Service (SBS) is one that hinges almost exclusively on selection rather than development and therefore lends itself to identifying those who can already perform at the highest level rather than those with the potential to develop. I suppose this has obvious benefits in an organisation where lives are at stake if people don't perform, but if organisations aren't careful this can come at the detriment of continuous improvement and innovation – both essential to sustained, elite performance. It's an easy argument – if there are only so many places available (typically five soldiers are successful for every 100 who are recommended by their units for selection), then we may as well take the last five standing at the end. There's no doubt that this approach guarantees a minimum standard, which for the SAS and the SBS is exceptionally high. The challenge then becomes maintaining their growth mindset and willingness to get even better. When you have put your body and mind on the line for six gruelling months of selection to eventually realise your lifetime ambition of becoming an SAS soldier, the message from their commanders has to be clear: 'Welcome to the family, but this is just the start.' It's not about being good enough to be here; it's about being good enough to do well here.

This simple point was beautifully illustrated by an address a commanding officer gave to his new recruits. He stood in front of them with three items lined up on a trestle table: a pair of boots, a rifle and a radio. 'What makes you successful in the Special Forces boils down to three commitments,' he explained. He pointed to the boots: 'You are fitter and stronger than anyone else.' He turned and pointed at the rifle: 'You can fire your rifle more accurately than anyone else.' He moved on to the radio: 'And you can communicate better than anyone else.'

His message was a simple and compelling reminder of what it means to live and breathe an Inside-Out mindset.

3
Failure: the victories within defeat

Imagine what it must be like to be a high-profile athlete in a renowned global sports team. Your mind probably goes straight to the feeling of winning, the financial reward and the adoration of millions of fans. Those fans scrutinise your performance week in, week out, as do the media. You've demonstrated what you are capable of and have worked hard to achieve it, but now the fans, media and even your teammates expect you to be the star of every game. When you are not, they can be scathing, and not just about your performance but also about you as a person. Now imagine missing a key shot in the final minute of the game to lose it for your team. It leaves your teammates, along with hundreds of thousands of fans, heartbroken. Now imagine finishing your career having had this very experience of last-minute failure repeated more times than any other player in history. How would you measure yourself? How would you judge your career?

Well, this did happen to a basketball player, and his name was Michael Jordan, star player for the Chicago Bulls in the late 1980s and 90s, as portrayed on the acclaimed Netflix documentary *The Last Dance*. His record for failing in the closing few moments of a game was matched by his record for success. He happened to make more last-minute shots to win the game than any other player in the history of the NBA and is almost universally considered to be one of the greatest athletes of all time. That is testament to his willingness to invest in loss along the path to being the best he could be.

Real champions give themselves up to the learning process. By doing this they have to be strong enough to take the psychological risk of failing in the short term in order to pursue continuous betterment.

This is a form of delayed gratification that every superstar has to grapple with on their way to the top, but we can all relate to the notion of short-term pain for long-term gain. Never has this been observed more vividly than in Stanford University's famous Marshmallow Test, in which kids sat in a room in front of a marshmallow for five minutes. If they got to the end without eating it, they would be given another one. This was a test of their ability to control their desire for immediate gratification in order to invest in the bigger picture.

Incredibly, this test is one of the best predictors of future success. But the truth is we all find it incredibly challenging to invest in future gains when we have the option of clinging on to the safety of what's in front of us.

In the marshmallow test you can generally spot from the outset the ones who are going to struggle and give in to temptation – they adopt a strategy of pure resistance, opening up a tension between logic and emotion. Our brain's emotional centre is far stronger than the areas responsible for rationale and reasoning, therefore if willpower is our only tactic, we are destined to fail. By contrast, the 'successful' children were visibly less resistant in their body language – sitting still, simply waiting for time to elapse. This seemed to be a different approach to willpower, less of a fight, more of a confident acknowledgement of the bigger picture.

We all like to imagine that we would think like Michael Jordan if we were blessed with the same potential, but the higher we climb, the more our fear of falling is tested. In this way, the better you get and the more your reputation precedes you, the greater the perceived risk of failure. It's easy to take a risk if you're a nobody; you have little to lose but a lot to gain. But when you start to build a reputation, you become invested in the idea of yourself as a somebody. At some point the desire to protect yourself grows stronger than the desire to challenge yourself further.

Jordan's story makes a compelling point about the importance of failure on the path to greatness. There is no doubt that those who haven't experienced losing routinely enough are emotionally unprepared. However, the message that 'we must fail in order to succeed' is not quite as simple as some might think and is open to gross mis-interpretation. I have seen schools introduce 'Failure Week' off the back of this message. The idea (I think) is that kids have to try new activities or practise existing ones to the point of failure. By making failure the goal here, I think they have missed an important point.

At no point did Jordan ever *try* to fail, or at least make failure an acceptable outcome. All the truly exceptional people I have worked with to date have one thing in common: failure feels like a disaster for them. They are ultra-competitive people who set the highest standards for themselves. They never enter the field of play wanting to do anything other than succeed in whatever endeavour they have set for themselves that day. The difference is, they know that failing is sometimes inevitable.

Prior to the 2012 London Olympics I was working with the Great Britain fencing team. I remember a specific session where the coach was teaching them a complex new move that involved hitting your opponent at very close quarters as they attack. It's an exceptionally difficult move to execute due to the combination of timing, athleti-cism and accuracy required. In the initial stages of training, I watched them repeat the sequence slowly and without an opponent, just so that they could focus wholly on correct technique. As elite athletes they picked it up remarkably quickly, soon demonstrating real grace and coordination. But then it was time to practise on each other.

The fencers were wired up against each other, meaning they were connected to the scoring system via a retractable wire, allowing for a bright light and buzzer to alarm as soon as one of the fencers made a hit on their opponent. For this particular exercise, one fencer was given the task of being the 'attacker' in order to allow their opponent to practise the new move. I soon noticed a familiar pattern of behav-iour play out across the whole team.

Initially, all fencers were struggling to successfully execute their new move, maybe because of timing, technique, accuracy or a com-bination of all of these. This was unsurprising given that this was their first attempt in full combat mode. This didn't stop their competitive instincts leading them to get a little frustrated. Despite this, I could see they were getting better and better with every attempt. Their technique was improving, and they were getting closer and closer to making the hit. But, on every attempt, all they saw and heard was their opponent's buzzer going off, indicating that they had lost the hit.

If at this point they had watched a video of themselves, measuring success in terms of technical improvement, they would have noticed how much they were getting better with every attempt. This would have fuelled their confidence to carry on. But by measuring success simply on whether they were beating their opponent, they were losing every time. This slowly eroded their confidence and diminished their sense of control. After they had made several more attempts and now just millimetres away from landing the hit, this became a brilliant test to see which athletes were focused Inside Out and which were Outside In.

By the end of the session, two thirds of the group had become so dispirited that they had given up and reverted to what they knew, claiming that the new move didn't suit their style of fencing. That was the Outside-In mindset talking. One third of the group, though, put the scores to one side as they focused on the mastery of what they were trying to do. Before each attempt they would be practising the move in their head, and after each attempt they would take a moment to process what just happened. That was the Inside-Out approach. Eventually, each of those athletes in this group achieved success, reinforcing their motivation for further mastery.

This was an astounding effect to witness. But what made it resonate even more was that one of these fencers went on to compete two weeks later at a World Cup competition. She achieved a personal-best result by beating one of the top-seeded opponents in the world, and ended up scoring her winning point using the move she had learned.

As a team we used this lesson to overcome an important mental hurdle. A hurdle that had been showing up in lots of different ways, and a hurdle that, up until this point, had held many of them back from reaching their potential. To truly learn and get better, you must give yourself up to the learning process. Put ego to one side while you pursue new skills and abilities, even if it means getting beaten. Without ego, the learning process has the potential to be frictionless.

If you fail to accept failure as part of the learning process, then the mechanism of learning, which you've relied on so heavily to get you where you are, starts to seize up. This becomes difficult to get going again.

What we learn from these stories is how easy it is to see success and failure as being synonymous with the result – the big hairy outcome. This makes it binary – we either succeed or we fail. In reality, our day is littered with mini-successes and failures.

The only reason Michael Jordan was even in a position to make the match-winning shot was because of a series of mini-successes that had led him to that point – his ability to win the ball in the first place, the three opponents he had managed to get past, the decision he had made to attack down a certain line. Each of these mini-successes was preceded by even smaller successes – he won the ball because he had jumped higher than his opponents, he had jumped higher because of a new strength regime he adopted three months ago, a regime he had adopted because of a book he read while exploring ways to get better. We have so many mini-successes and failures that we don't notice most of them, let alone appreciate them as successes, but it's important that we do. It's thanks to all of these mini-successes that Jordan created the opportunity to fail in the first place.

In a culture preoccupied with results, people are in danger of neglecting the very things – and people – that enable those results to happen. In a culture that notices and rewards only the outcome of people's behaviours rather than the behaviours themselves, people are likely to develop a sense of learned helplessness – feeling like instruments in someone else's process. High-performing cultures are quick to recognise the small victories that encourage specific behaviours to be repeated, because without them the big victories simply cannot happen.

Next time you find yourself in a position where you have the opportunity to succeed or fail, ask yourself what mini-successes led you to that amazing opportunity.

4

Focus: thinking under pressure

The pressure to perform at our best conjures up plenty of weird and wonderful effects on our mind and body, effects that make even the most routined and well-practised of skills remarkably challenging when we have an audience, an expectation to deliver results, or severe consequences to failing. This explains why the best footballers in the world might step up to take a penalty and miss the goal entirely, or why we might stand up in front of an audience and completely forget how to talk normally. These examples further reinforce an uncomfortable truth: that practice alone is not enough. Physical repetition will never prepare us fully for the lived reality of being in that situation. But why not? And how do we train for these eventualities?

Mental strategies for high-pressure moments require us to address two components of our inner game: one is our emotional and physiological response, and the other is our mental response – more specifically – how we focus our attention. It's this mental side we will focus on here, but we will take plenty of time to explore our emotional and physiological response in the Feeling Dimension where we train our ability to stay calm and relaxed in stressful situations.

In much of life, focus is a 'nice to have'. We know it's valuable for most day-to-day tasks and activities, but losing focus isn't such a big issue; we might complete tasks a little slower and with a few more mistakes, but it's nothing to lose sleep over. Yet your ability to focus – to narrow your attention on what is really important in any given moment or period of time – has far-reaching consequences for the way you deal with life's toughest challenges.

On 4 September 2010, an earthquake measuring 7.1 in magnitude rocked the city of Christchurch in New Zealand. Buildings shook violently, power was lost entirely and water mains burst. In this particular earthquake no one was killed, but the region suffered a prolonged threat of aftershocks. At this time a researcher from the University of Christchurch noticed the impact it was having on people's behaviour. While some citizens found themselves responding positively to the stress, rallying round and being super-productive, others were suddenly paralysed with indecision, forgetting appointments and unable to concentrate at work.

Interested in the implications of disasters on human performance, Deak Helton and his colleagues set about trying to understand what was going on here, and what differentiated the more resilient citizens from their less resilient compatriots.

Before I share their findings, I want to explain the two broad modes in which your brain operates in response to meaningful situations. Firstly, there is the 'threat-avoidance' mode where you focus on what could go wrong and how to avoid it. Secondly, there is the 'reward-approach' mode where you focus on opportunity and how to move towards it. All of us are operating according to the interplay of these two systems, which rise and fall in different situations according to our sensitivity to threat and reward. So profound are these two modes of operating that psychologist Jeffrey Grey described every human being as being the protagonist in a perpetual struggle between reward-approach and punishment-avoidance. Like two completely different software programs, when you run them you get very different results.[1]

Threat–avoidance mode

We've all been in that situation where we are scared to have a go for fear of failing and being exposed for being worse than people thought we were. In this moment your brain has done a complex calculation and come to a simple conclusion – the threat of trying and failing is greater than the reward for trying and succeeding. In this case the brain flicks into a mode that neuroscientists describe as threat-avoidance.

This mode initiates a set of behaviours linked to caution, inhibition and protectionism. When you focus on the threat, your limbic system slams into overdrive, galvanising an extreme stress response while simultaneously stealing valuable resources from the frontal cortex, thereby preventing you from thinking clearly. Your attention diverts to anything that you perceive as harmful – the expectant look of the audience in front of you or the memories of what happened last time you were here. This is known as cortical inhibition and is the reason you may make uncharacteristic mistakes under pressure, mistakes you would never normally make in training or practice.

Reward–approach mode

The alternative is reward-approach, when your mindset is geared more towards the reward of success rather than the threat of failure. To get here you might need to be conscious of how you re-frame the pressure of 'big-match' situations. I have heard many athletes and business leaders talk about the privilege of being under pressure. For example, a golfer taking a pressure putt on the 18th green to win the Masters might reframe what could easily be an overwhelming experience by reminding himself that he has worked hard to create this opportunity for himself. It's an opportunity that very few others have experienced, so he may as well embrace the challenge!

In reward-approach mode you will lean *into* the situation rather than *away* from it. It is therefore linked to passionate and go-getting behaviour. At a Premier League Football conference I was intrigued to learn of a study that found that in nations more successful at penalty-taking, players tended to place the ball down and walk backwards – facing the goalkeeper. In nations less successful at penalties, players were more likely to place the ball down and then turn their back on the goalkeeper as they walked back for their run-up. My guess would be that this is a physical manifestation of threat-avoidance and reward-approach modes. It signals a confidence, I suppose, that the player is leaning into the situation, not leaning away from it. If you turn your back, it might suggest that there's a threat that you are trying to avoid. It's a behaviour that parallels neatly with the findings of most neuroscientists.

I know what you might be thinking, 'Why not just tell a player to walk backwards after placing the ball on the spot?' This will sadly not make them better at taking penalties. This is because their inner experience is more dominant in predicting their outer behaviours – not the other way round. In other words, you need that player to actually *feel* confident – rather than just act confidently. There is evidence to suggest that acting confidently can help you to feel more confident, but this might be very fragile in the face of immense pressure.

This takes us back to New Zealand, where it turns out that this interplay between threat-avoidance and punishment-reward was important for understanding the very different reactions from Christchurch citizens following the earthquake. As part of the study they tested all participants in a basic focus exercise called the 'Sustained Attention to Response Test' (SART), only to find that the group who maintained their everyday effectiveness after the earthquake also scored more highly on the SART. After further investigation they concluded that 'focus' was a key determinant of their ability to overcome adversity. This was reinforced by the fact that the more resilient participants seemed to be good at setting small, everyday goals which allowed them to stay task-focused and positive.

In contrast, where participants had less structure and poorly defined goals, their mind was more likely to wander. More specifically their minds would wander back to the threat of further tremors. This is because a stressful mind is more likely to gravitate towards unhappy and threatening thoughts. Importantly, this does not necessarily suggest that resilient people ignore threat; rather they are likely to be more deliberate in how (and when) they address it. They don't allow a wandering mind to replay negative thoughts over and over.

The key thing here is that you have a choice on where you place your attention – even though it doesn't always feel like it. When it comes to focus, the key to success is in exercising this choice. The New Zealand study confirmed what neuroscientists had long suspected: that, left to chance, our mind will wander towards whatever makes us feel most threatened, which for many people in performance environments is the fear of failure. The higher the stakes the greater the threat, therefore training your brain to be good at pressure requires you to be more conscious and deliberate in how you direct your attention towards positive, meaningful goals.[2]

Refocus

Whenever you feel yourself losing your composure, practise this simple refocus exercise. In the first place, you must get good at noticing when your thoughts are hazy, rushed or negative. Maybe you are repeating the same mistakes or not getting the response you are looking for from the situation.

When this happens commit to the following 'Press Pause' exercise:

1 Step 1: Press pause.
   Stop what you are doing and, if possible, extract yourself from the immediacy of the situation. Take five deep, relaxing breaths. Focus on the quality of these breaths, nothing else. If you need longer to settle your mind and body, take longer.

2 Step 2: What's happening?
   Ask yourself, 'What am I noticing here?' Don't just notice what's going on around you, also notice what is happening on the inside (e.g. 'I am allowing myself to get frustrated and as a result I am rushing or shutting down').

3 Step 3: What do I want to happen?
   Clarify what exactly you want to achieve from this situation.

4 Step 4: What do I need to change?
   Now that you have clarified your intent, what can you change in order to get there? (e.g. slow down and be patient).

Following this exercise you should be able to continue what you were doing with renewed focus and clarity. You will also notice that the more you practise, the quicker and more effectively your mind will adjust. This is the benefit of treating it as a training exercise.

Keep it simple

In performance terms, pressure serves to activate and heighten our senses through our stress response. In order for this to help us rather than hinder us, we need *focus*. This means that high performance is a careful interplay between optimising pressure and maximizing focus. In other words, it's not pressure that effects your performance, it's your ability to control your attention under pressure. Perhaps the most important principle for achieving this is to keep things simple.

In the midst of intense pressure moments, our working memory is reduced – this is the amount of information we can hold in our mind at one point in time. This is often why athletes struggle to transfer complex skills from the training ground into competition – they don't have the processing power to control as much as they might be able to when not under pressure. The goal is therefore to manage what you give yourself to focus on such that you are challenged enough to utilise your full working memory, but not so challenged that your working memory 'floods' and you become overwhelmed. Therefore, as a general rule for high-pressure situations, I have found that people respond best to having a simple focus with total commitment. This has informed my own personal mantra – 'simple principles applied world-class!'

Performing in your bubble

At the very heart of performance psychology is the concept of 'control the controllables'. I imagine this is probably the most commonly repeated mantra in performance psychology. It has become so simple to say – yet so hard to do. This is because understanding this principle intellectually is not enough; it needs to become part of how you think automatically.

Here's an exercise you might wish to try: thinking of a particularly challenging situation that you might find yourself in over the next few weeks or months, draw a large circle on a piece of paper. This is your bubble. As long as you are performing in your bubble, you are focused on all the things you can, and want, to control in relation to this pressure situation. If you are outside your bubble, it means you are occupying yourself with the things you can't control.

Therefore, outside the bubble, write down all the things you can't control that may play on your mind as you move closer to this particular event. Once you have taken time to do that, turn your attention to the inside where you will write down all the things that you can and want to control in this situation. Really try to think of everything that might be going on for you.

As you sit back to admire your bubble, what do you notice? Hopefully you notice and appreciate the logic of what you see written down in front of you. Figure 4.1 is a generic example of what your bubble might look like. This illustrates the rational 'logic' of what is happening, thereby nurturing an Inside-Out response to pressure. In other words, it should encourage you to invest your attention in the elements you can control within the bubble.

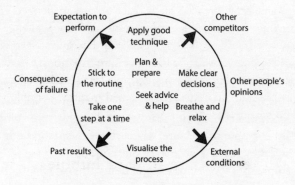

FIGURE 4.1 The reality of the situation

What seems like a very rational thought process when we see it on paper becomes highly distorted in our head. Why? Whereas the data on the inside are processed largely by the frontal lobe of the rational brain, the data on the outside have the potential to be much more threatening (largely because they are very meaningful but we can't control them) and therefore they are picked up by the limbic system of the emotional brain, driving our stress response. Remember, these emotional data resonate about five times more than the rational data. Therefore, for your uncensored mind, your perception of a high-challenge situation is more like that illustrated in Figure 4.2, where the emotional 'charge' of what's on the outside is five times greater than what's on the inside.

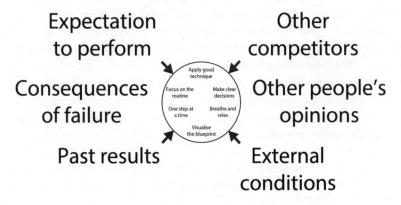

Expectation to perform

Other competitors

Apply good technique

Focus on the routine

Make clear decisions

One step at a time

Breathe and relax

Visualise the blueprint

Consequences of failure

Other people's opinions

Past results

External conditions

FIGURE 4.2 How your brain perceives the same situation

The extent of this emotional charge is based on the commonly held belief of neuroscientists that our emotional brain is five times stronger than our rational brain. This is far from an exact science; nonetheless it makes the point that we are all highly susceptible to an Outside-In response to pressure, where suddenly we find our mental acuity tainted by matters outside of our control.

This emphasises the importance of doing this exercise on paper in order to reinforce your rational thinking. The goal is not to ignore the information on the outside (we know from our first principle of positive psychology at the beginning of the chapter that we can't do this); rather it's to focus wholly on what's on the inside. The importance of writing down the things you can't control on the outside is because, by acknowledging them, it is easier to accept them. It's this capacity to *accept* what you can't control that allows you to tune into what you can control – one requires the other. You effectively disarm what's on the outside so that it can no longer compete in the same way with what's on the inside. You can now channel your energy into what is within your control.

This sounds easy, but your mind will wander. Meditation becomes a useful tool to help with this, and it also teaches you how to accept negative thoughts without holding on to them. The goal of meditation is to simply observe your thoughts – not to *be* your thoughts. Think of your thoughts travelling through your mind on a conveyer belt, coming and going in and out of your consciousness. You have good thoughts and you have bad thoughts – no one is any different in that respect. The only difference is which thoughts you pick up and play with. These are the thoughts you feed and give meaning to.

When I am working with people on their bubbles, we sometimes find it helpful to create a script with positive statements that help to reinforce this principle:

> I accept and let go of anything I can't control including the outcome – this will take care of itself. I can always think about it later – no problem – but for now I will place what I cannot control outside of my bubble. Now, within my bubble I have all the space and time I need. I am free and clear in mind to focus on what I will control. I am well prepared, and I will stay focused on one step at a time. This is simple, and I know it works. By staying calm and focused on these simple things it will lead me to where I want to go. With the nervous energy I may feel in my body I will channel it into my routine, one step at a time. Trust the process.

If you want to respond positively and effectively every time to high-pressure situations then you cannot rely on tools and techniques that you only ever apply once in a while on the big occasion. A golfer wouldn't suddenly change their swing technique because they felt the pressure to take a good shot, in the same way that a surgeon wouldn't suddenly change their technique and procedures just because they felt the pressure of a life-saving surgery. This is the same for your mental approach – if you want to be good at it when you need it, it needs to be part of your everyday way of thinking. Whether it's competitive situations, chairing a meeting, taking exams, performing in front of large audiences, be alive to the opportunity to practise this all the time.

Remember that your ability to maintain clarity in your mind alongside intensity in the body boils down to how you have strengthened and organised the appropriate pathways in your brain over time. Getting your thoughts in order and making the right connections as part of your day-to-day training process is exactly what we cover in the second half of the Thinking Dimension where we turn our attention towards our mental aptitude.

5
Belief: it's all in the head

When I was 16 I made the difficult choice to study chemistry as part of my higher-level education. It was never a subject I found particularly easy but I knew it was an important stepping stone on the path I wanted to take (which was to become a horse-racing forensic scientist!). I remember turning up at the first class and the teacher telling us that, in order to understand more advanced chemistry, we would do well to forget most of what we had been taught up until that point. The news didn't go down well with many, especially for those whose idea of being good at chemistry was being able to recite the periodic table backwards.

I have since realised that the message the teacher was trying to convey was one that resonates in all high-performing environments. On the path to excellence you routinely have to challenge and let go of things you are familiar with in order to succeed at the next level up. As a result, you have to really believe in what you are doing, believe in your system, believe in those around you and, most importantly, believe in yourself.

Out of principle, I have never asked someone to practise a technique that I haven't practised myself. This is important because it allows me to appreciate the leap of faith I am asking them to take, having taken it once myself. What I hadn't always appreciated was the extent to which our *belief* in a person, a technique or an intervention can be more powerful than the intervention itself. In medical circles this is called the placebo effect, but the science of mind over body has implications that stretch well beyond medicine. Indeed, belief is the universal currency for all elite performers.

The placebo effect

In medical terms, the placebo effect is when an improvement in symptoms is observed, despite using a non-active treatment, such as using a sugar pill rather than an active drug. The placebo effect is an inconvenient truth for traditional medicine and pharmaceutical companies which rely on the efficacy of the drugs they produce. The idea that the positive effects of their drugs may be driven by the beliefs of the person taking them rather than by the drug itself could be very threatening.

It's taken a long time, but Western medicine is now starting to come round to the role that belief plays in the efficacy of medical practice. Pioneering research into the placebo effect has shed light on evidence that belief is the primary mechanism by which many medications have their effect, especially in treatments for areas such as depression, anxiety and sleep. The science of placebo pills is very specific. Large pills work better than small pills, blue pills are better for sleep and anxiety, and red pills are better for relieving pain.

The placebo effect seems to be particularly prominent for things like pain, fatigue, anxiety and depression. This suggests that the way we manage our minds plays an important role in regulating the chemical balance in the brain, and that the mere expectation that something will work unlocks the mechanisms that effect real change. Amazingly, there is a still a placebo effect even if the patient knows it is just a placebo – so long as the doctor who prescribes it believes it will still help them!

Unsurprisingly, the placebo effect has huge implications in the world of high performance, where in pushing yourself to the limit you expose your vulnerabilities, and with that you question what you really believe. On the plus side, this helps to explain why positive expectation is so essential in a high-performance setting and why optimism is such a universal trait among resilient individuals.

In many ways, our growing understanding of the power of placebo shouldn't come as a surprise to us. There has always been evidence of our ability to access and connect with our more intuitive mechanisms for pain control, mood regulation and focus. Indeed, anyone who has been told by a great coach or mentor, 'I believe in you – now believe in yourself', will appreciate the impact that belief has on their ability to find another level.

There are also techniques such as hypnosis which work on the power of suggestion, something we have known about for some time when it comes to changing unhelpful beliefs, but also in controlling our perception of pain. It has become commonplace for people to undergo surgical procedures under hypnosis, using no medical pain relief. Hypno-birthing is a great example of this. It turns out that patients hypnotised before surgery suffer fewer complications and recover faster as well as experiencing less pain. I have spoken to surgeons who were very much aligned to the traditional Western models of medicine before, and are now far more accommodating of this practice for their patients, even though it must be a little nerve-wracking for them if they have been used to injecting patients with painkillers.

Scientists studying bio-resilience have shown that our state of mind can trigger molecular changes deep inside our cells. In the relatively new field of epigenetics, this can even influence how our DNA is expressed. Mechanisms are being uncovered all the time linking our thoughts and behaviours to our cellular biology. This has brought new life to the 'nature or nurture' debate. Scientists now generally accept the notion that nature loads the gun and nurture pulls the trigger.

Anchored confidence

The most powerful of all the beliefs we own is the belief we have in our *self.*

Research leaves us in no doubt about the correlation between high confidence and high performance. But statisticians will be cautious about any interpretation that one causes the other. To test this for yourself, let's do a quick thought experiment... Which comes first for you, confidence or performance? In other words, do you need to be confident in order to perform well? Or do you need to perform well in order to feel confident? If you find it difficult to untangle these two, you are not the only one.

I will not be so bold as to suggest there is a 'right' answer to this. I have, however, asked hundreds of elite performers this question, from SAS soldiers to world sporting champions, and from surgeons to successful entrepreneurs, and there is definitely a high level of agreement among them all: they have to perform well in order to feel truly confident. Explaining why, many of them differentiated *deep* confidence from *superficial* confidence. It is not good enough to pretend to be confident.

Acting like Muhammad Ali will not help you fight like Muhammad Ali. Or, if it does, it will last only until you get punched in the face. True confidence comes from a deep sense of control that must be built over time. Another way of putting it is that you cannot lead with confidence if there are no core beliefs backing it up – and it's difficult to establish core beliefs about your ability without being able to reference your successes – no matter how small or incremental they may be.

It's this anchored confidence that allows you to get out of your own way – to focus less on how you are doing and more on the task in front of you, being there in the moment. It's at this point that you are capable of listening and not just speaking, showing vulnerability as well as strength, having the courage to change the plan if things aren't working, as well as the courage to stay committed to the plan when things get tough. It is when you are most confident that you are able to bring all your human qualities to one place at the same time.

Nowhere is this more true than in a court of law. Here it is the role of highly skilled barristers to cross-examine witnesses and defendants. You may well have familiarised yourself with this environment through hit TV shows like *Suits*. Where there is a clear outcome – guilty or not guilty – there will always be a winner and a loser. Like any athlete, barristers are used to winning and losing. But, unlike an athlete, in the justice system winning and losing is not meant to be in the control of the lawyers regardless of how good they are; it is meant to be governed by the facts of the case. Inevitably, these facts are sometimes stacked in one side's favour. Despite this the cross-examiner must still do their job to the best of their ability even if they know that the case might be almost impossible for them to win. One would hope that the right decision is made every time, but the reality is that the courtroom itself provides a competitive, high-stakes arena for well-trained and very skilled people who take pride in the work they do. If a lawyer's lack of self-belief and confidence starts to erode their ability to establish the truth, then proportionate justice becomes more difficult to achieve. In other words, the system works best when *everyone* is at their best.

This poses an interesting dilemma: if your performance is intrinsically tied up in your belief and confidence, how do you perform at your best when winning or losing is out of your hands? I've posed this question to a number of barristers I've worked alongside, some of whom are regularly cross-examining in high-profile murder trials, How do they evoke belief to do their job to the best of their ability when the facts are skewed so heavily against them?

I am reminded of a simple definition of confidence: confidence is the answer to the question 'Can I do it?' Your answer will almost exclusively depend on what 'it' is. In the case of a barrister, if 'it' is winning every case, they will end up having an inconsistent relationship with what they can control – this can lead to learned helplessness and low self-belief. If instead 'it' is their quality of preparation leading up to the case, their research, notes, case familiarisation, practice, time management, turning up well rested, staying focused, and so on, then there are multiple anchors for belief and confidence. Interestingly, barristers all describe how their belief in their ability to achieve a successful outcome in court is actually shaped by how well they attend to the small things – almost like they are collecting confidence tokens along the way until eventually they have enough tokens to invest in the outcome. But, regardless of the result, they can take pride in the fact that they have done everything they can – that's all they can do. They will be a more skilful and successful barrister for doing it like this.

This point was reinforced for me during an insightful conversation I had during a leadership programme for UK Special Forces. I was working with a small team of soldiers, and we were debating this very question of confidence and performance. They came to the conclusion that, in their experience, confidence was an output of doing other things well. They trust deeply in their training, but just as importantly, they need to have unwavering confidence in one another. They need to know that those around them have the knowledge, the skills and the temperament to do their job to the highest standard.

Out of curiosity I dug a bit deeper, and what I noticed was that the conversation kept coming back to one theme that under-pinned this confidence – predictability. This I found interesting because people don't generally aspire to be more predictable. It's not a quality we typically aim for. But in critical missions that are complex, dangerous and volatile, predictability is exactly what they need from one another. It's problematic enough not knowing what the enemy is going to do, but it's much more so not knowing what your own teammates are going to do. Only by sharing the same mental models for how they solve problems and make decisions, the same tactics, the same operating procedures and the same values are they able to create layers of predictability in an otherwise chaotic environment. It was this, they argued, that gave them confidence.

Positive thinking or just positive talking?

High performers are congruent in their thoughts, feelings and actions. By this I mean that what they express consciously is com-pletely aligned to what they believe subconsciously.

I have met countless athletes who have said that they wanted to win a gold medal. But, as they said it, their eyes, body language and tone of voice suggested otherwise. The words they said were clearly incongruent with how they really felt and therefore how they behaved. The danger here is that we are constantly being encouraged to think positively and say positive things, but without anchoring it in any meaningful way to the true beliefs we have about ourselves or our abilities.

Very often you may be culturally motivated to say the 'right' things in order to appease managers, sponsors, investors, coaches and parents. In doing so, you isolate yourself further and further from the truth of your inner experience. High performers rely on this con-gruence to be able to perform with freedom. Performance is a form of self-expression that relies on the inner world being connected and congruent with the outer world. When you watch mind-blowing performances from musicians on stage, comedians making their audience laugh, inspirational speakers making their audience cry, you are experiencing an expression of their inner state that you unconsciously feel compelled to mirror. You feel what they are feeling. How can you bring other people with you if you are not congruent within yourself?

I worry for the many politicians who fall into the incongruence trap. They have been conditioned by the media to believe that they are weak if they don't have an answer to everything. They are also weak if they do have an answer but later decide to change their mind. And the ultimate weakness is to show emotion – *any* emotion. The importance of being 'correct' every time leads them into a game of charades, justifying policies and decisions that turn out to be flawed.

Politicians know better than most of us that we live in an imperfect world, yet they are not allowed to acknowledge or express this imperfection. Since they are not granted permission to be wrong, they have developed sophisticated survival techniques which largely involve deflection. They end up having to focus harder on these survival techniques than on the policies themselves. This can be exhausting, as you will know if you have ever had to work in an organisation where you felt the constant need to defend, justify or protect your-*self*. This leads us nicely to the next chapter where we explore how our identity and personal brand help shape our success.

6

Identity: the story you tell yourself about yourself

Many ambitious people have failed to reach their potential not due to any lack of skill or ability but because they struggle to identify with being that person who is successful, who stands on the podium with a gold medal around their neck or at the boardroom table offering real value and leadership. The most common form of this is called imposter syndrome, when you doubt yourself in the role you're in and feel that you're going to be found out as a fraud.

In a fascinating study conducted in Toronto,[1] students were asked to summarise a passage about statistical methods in less than two minutes. They were told that the topic was standard knowledge in the field. What the students didn't know was that the passage was deliberately written in a way that was ambiguous and didn't make sense. The time pressure and the implausibility of the task made them feel uncertain, frustrated and confused, and therefore threatened. The key question was: how did they react to the threat?

Researchers measured their brain activity in response to the task, In particular they wanted to find out whether the students adopted a 'threat-avoidant' profile of activity or a 'reward-approach' profile. It turned out that many of the students reacted as expected to this threat – moving towards a threat-avoidant profile in their brain activity. But others actually showed a massive increase in reward-approach activity in their brain despite having been presented with the same threat. What was different about this sub-group?

Take a moment to think whether you agree with these statements:

- I can do things as well as most other people.
- I feel I have quite a lot to be proud of.
- I take a positive attitude towards myself.

This is a simple way of measuring self-esteem. If you answer no to questions like these, your self-esteem is lower. If you answer yes, your self-esteem is higher. Students with low self-esteem were the ones who showed greater avoidance activity in the brain, but the students with high self-esteem showed a dramatically opposite pattern with increases in the reward–approach areas of the brain. This suggests that they were approaching or confronting the threats. As neuroscientist Professor Ian Robertson neatly puts it, 'You need to respect yourself ... if you are to benefit from stress through your brain rising to the challenge rather than shrinking from threat.'[2]

Some of the most influential thoughts we have are therefore thoughts we have about our self and our self-worth. Since the dawn of humanity, the question 'Who am I?' has been the central tenet for many philosophers, presumably because the answer influences everything we think and feel about our place in the world.

In my work with top performers, I notice they are not afraid to lean into these more existential questions. Exercising this part of their mind helps them to eliminate self-doubt and shields them from the external pressures they are routinely subject to, especially if they have celebrity status (something which is often an uninvited consequence of being good at what they do). For this reason, it also helps for them to have an inner circle of people they can trust and practise talking openly with.

Relentless ambition

Our sense of identity is very often the hardest driver of ambition. The idea of being a surgeon may be more exciting than actually doing surgery; the idea of being a top footballer may be more compelling than actually playing football every day. Who we are is wrapped up in what we do, and what we do is wrapped up in who we are. This can work for us or against us. Having worked with some of London's leading law firms, often referred to as 'Magic Circle' firms, I have noticed this to be particularly true of corporate lawyers. When people have trained exceptionally hard to be where they are, often having to overcome many hurdles along the way, they become so invested that it's hard to disentangle who they are from what they do. This particular breed of lawyers are phenomenally committed – they work unbelievably long hours.

As an outsider, you're taken aback by how status drives almost every conversation inside a law firm. There's definitely a pecking order that unconsciously plays out in every interaction. It can be extreme, but it appeals to that human condition of rising to the top. Nearly every lawyer below partner level wants to become a partner, sometimes to the point of obsession – the financial rewards are disproportionately large compared with those of a senior associate at the level below, yet so too are the pressure and expectation. For many lawyers, their identity is where they sit in the hierarchy – this is the measure of their value and, for many, of their success.

In reality, you have many 'selves'. At work I may be a lawyer, a manager, a team member, a client, an advisor and a mentor. Out of work I may be a wife, a mother, a daughter, a sister, a friend, a musician, a runner, a volunteer – you get the picture. You invest in many 'selves', and you may invest more energy in some and less in others.

I notice this in high-powered career people. Every decision in life has been made for their career. By channelling their focus and investment in one direction they inadvertently alienate themselves from other concerns and pursuits like family, friends, hobbies and wellbeing.

By channelling all your energy into a single pursuit there is no doubt you progress more fervently towards it. At least initially. The reward might be achievement, status, power and wealth (not necessarily in that order). But there is a potential dark side to this. Limiting the number of identities you invest in has unintended consequences. Over time you starve yourself of the unique richness that comes from the variety and perspective you get from these different investments – love, compassion, health, humour, trust, bravery, humility. It's this richness of human experience that fertilises the biology of resilience, and you will never get all of these things from one identity.

In addition, investing all you have in one 'self' has another consequence. I heard one ambitious lawyer say, 'If I fail as a lawyer, I fail as a person – at least this is how it can feel.' This may sound extreme, but it's how many people feel in these environments even if they don't say it out loud. Understandably, this leads to a pronounced fear of failure. The easiest coping mechanism for this is limiting opportunities to fail, which in turn means limiting opportunities to learn and get better. This becomes a vicious circle – in wanting it so badly on the outside I end up limiting my progression on the inside.

This is a dimension of human character that can be quite extreme in high-performance environments; nonetheless, you must avoid the temptation to label it as good or bad. By being 'all in', fully invested in your goals, it makes you 100 per cent committed and determined, which is a prerequisite for success. But this also makes it difficult to separate results from self-worth. In addition, an unhealthy attachment to the outcome affects your capacity to let go of mistakes, to work effectively in teams, to demonstrate compassion and inspire loyalty in others, and to separate small problems from the big picture.

Even for the most ardent of high achievers there is always a balance to be had, and most of us spend a whole career trying to find it. While we do that, here are a few simple coaching questions that should help you find your own balance. I tend to use these questions on a regular basis because people's answers change over time.

- Why is this goal so important to me?
- What are my assumptions about what it will be like to achieve it?
- How will I know this goal continues to be good for me?
- Who else will be affected by this?
- What different identities are important to me along the way?
- How do I define success in each of these?
- Therefore how will I maintain a balance across these identities?

Section 2: Mental aptitude: performing intelligently

'If you are not willing to learn, no one can help you. If you are determined to learn, no one can stop you.'

Zig Ziglar

7
Learning: improve faster than your opponents

It strikes me that when you embark upon a new venture, activity or career you have a unique opportunity to shape your approach to excellence. It is at this point that you are often at your most excited, most open-minded and most optimistic for your success. In the next few pages I want to share with you the mental processes that have allowed my clients to build and train the architecture of their mind such that they are able to channel this energy and optimism into achieving superhuman results.

To be the best in the world you must learn faster than your opponents. It takes less than a minute to travel down the mountain in the sport of skeleton, navigating 15–20 corners along the way. The physical pressure on a skeleton athlete's body is significant, and partly for this reason athletes will 'slide' only twice per day. Any more than that and they will start to experience diminishing returns, both mentally and physically.

This equates to 1 minute 56 seconds of training every day. Hardly very much practice to become an expert. In his book *Outliers*, Malcolm Gladwell helped to popularise the work of Anders Ericcson, Professor of Psychology at Florida State University, and his notion of 10,000 hours of deliberate practice.[1] The 'rule' suggests that it takes 10,000 hours of intensive practice to achieve mastery of complex skills like playing a violin or computer programming. If this were true for Lizzy Yarnold, then it would have taken her approximately 600 years to reach the level she did. Clearly, we didn't have that long, which meant we had to think very differently.

Importantly, the 10,000 hours rule states that the practice must be 'deliberate', an essential detail that often gets overlooked. Therefore understanding the process and psychology for deliberate practice was something we examined long and hard within the skeleton team. Our objective was simple – in order to be the best team in the world on the track we would also have to be the best team in the world at learning off the track.

So how did we address this challenge of accelerated learning? Well, with a little help from Aldous Huxley, an English novelist and philosopher, and the author of *Brave New World*. He is credited with one of my favourite quotes. 'Experience is not what happens to a man; it is what a man does with what happens to him.'

Deliberate practice implies that there is more to becoming an expert than simply repetition. If you rely solely on this, then very soon *useful* repetition turns into *mindless* repetition. Take driving, for example. Most people are more than capable of driving to pass their test and get their licence. The learning journey continues as you gain more experience. By driving regularly, maybe in different cars and in different conditions, you reinforce your driving pathways in the brain until it becomes second nature. Now you have become an intuitive driver, you are driving without conscious effort. Does this mean you are world-class at driving? You might think so, but the answer is no! Does it qualify you to race against the best in the world? Of course not. At some point your learning has tailed off – not because you are as good as you can be, but because you have stopped applying deliberate practice.

Over a longer timescale, this could be the difference between an individual who has had 20 years' experience in their industry compared with someone who has had one year of experience repeated 20 times. It's how you learn from your experience that is so important in helping you improve and be better at what you do. We are taught that practice makes perfect, when in fact practice makes permanent. Only perfect practice can make perfect. For the best in the world, it's the *quality* of their practice that sets them apart, not necessarily the *amount*.

Inspired by the Huxley quotation, we looked at every aspect of the skeleton team's training, with the most focus ending up on what they did before and after the practice run itself (there's only so much you can tell an athlete to do in 58 seconds!). Each individual became an expert at managing their mental and physical state before training, visualising the challenges they were about to undertake and the skills they were about to use. Essential to this process was also working on memory recall – if a slider got to the bottom of the mountain unable to accurately make sense of what just happened, they had effectively lost half a day's training.

These challenges are not unique to skeleton; indeed, they are not unique to sport. They are principles which underpin high-performance learning in any environment. The only difference in skeleton is that we had to be explicit about our principles for learning rather than treat them as an after-thought or a nice-to-have. It's these principles I want to share in this part of the book on mental aptitude.

We can all get better at how we apply intelligence to our craft. Within the skeleton team it was something which we were committed to training through a process of accelerated learning. To do this well we would all (coaches and athletes) have to become experts in critical thinking, pattern recognition, performance conversations, feed-forward and feedback. Any weakness in these areas could have negated a whole day's training for the athletes, or at least slowed down their capacity to learn and improve.

This has huge implications for businesses and industries which expect their workforce to 'learn on the job', a concept that tends to be done passively rather than actively.

My approach to accelerated learning is anchored in neuroscience. The reason for this is simple: learning is a function of what happens in your brain. Neurons (brain cells) connect and strengthen to form neural pathways – highways of energy in the brain that correspond to complex skills, behaviours and thought processes. Your ability is contingent on how well adapted these skills, behaviours and thought processes are to the task at hand.

This ability of the brain to change and adapt in response to learning new skills is called neuroplasticity, something which is available to all of us, no matter how old we are. We all have the ability to improve incrementally at anything. How good we end up being is a function of time, focus and engagement, but of course there will always be limitations in our hardware – someone who is five foot three inches tall will never make an Olympic rowing team! Nonetheless, the opportunity to get better is always available to us. Maintained over time this can produce some surprising results.

Importantly for our skeleton athletes, the speed at which neural pathways can form and strengthen is a function of the training protocol. In particular, we explored three key principles of accelerated learning in order to maximise the speed at which the athletes adapted compared with their rivals:

- repetition
- making the right connections
- making it resonate.

All three of these are important in reaching our potential. As we learn more about them you will realise that they are simple in essence, but there is a host of reasons why these principles can go wrong in practice. I will also be sharing the main pitfalls to avoid.

It's probably worth noting at this point that reinforcing new connections and pathways in the brain is phenomenally energy intensive. Hence, if you are committed to this process, you must decide how much energy you are prepared to use because you simply can't apply the same intensity to everything you do. That said, if you're anything like me, it's less about being world-class at everything you turn your hand to and more about getting a return on your energy investment for the effort you choose to apply. Regardless, you will need plenty of recovery time, with good sleep and good nutrition, if you want to learn faster than the rest.

8

Repetition: practice makes permanent

If you want to get better at something, you have to practise. This simple fact isn't up for debate. We now know that repetition on its own isn't enough to become an expert, but this doesn't make repetition any less important. It is still an essential ingredient for success – and there is a science to doing it well.

In the section on mental attitude, we explored how practice often starts as a highly engaging activity. Like a child at play, it's fun. We are not necessarily doing it with the end in mind; rather, we are simply enjoying the process of learning for enjoyment's sake. Continue this indefinitely and, at some point, what started as something that was fun turns into more of a discipline.

I remember learning to play the piano at school when I was ten. Along with all the school's other musicians I was sent down to the 'practice rooms' during break time every day. This was an underground labyrinth of tiny rooms with no windows and no air. We were effectively incarcerated in these rooms for 45 minutes at a time to practise. The corridors were patrolled by a member of staff who would make sure we didn't escape. I always felt sorry for them for having to listen to the cacophony of horrific noises coming from the dozens of rooms that lined the corridor – I'm sure it would have been considered torture in many cultures.

Looking back on it now, I can see that we were never taught how to practise. We were told *what* to practise, but never *how* to practise. I now realise how limiting this was. Eventually, like most of the other kids, I gave up my musical instrument, something which most teachers and parents would consider normal at some point. But if only I knew then what I know now I think I would have applied myself very differently. And had more fun in the process.

Mindless repetition or mindful practice?

I enjoy asking people of all skills and abilities: 'Why do you practise?' Very often people talk about 'clocking up the hours' and 'building muscle memory', ideas which are easily misinterpreted.

To help guide your thinking around these interpretive trip hazards, it's important to remember the role the brain plays in all of this. Muscle memory, for example, does not exist in the muscle. The memory for skilled movement exists in the brain. It is the brain that executes your actions – your muscles are simply the instruments it uses. This is important to remember because the brain is open to other sorts of influences that determine how clear the signal is that it's sending to the muscles. Your mood and your quality of focus are just two examples of influencers that affect your ability to access the right pathways. This is called mood–state congruence and makes it essential to learn a skill in the mental state in which you intend to apply that skill.

Before any activity that you are trying to progress or get better at, always take time to breathe, relax your muscles and clear your mind. You might listen to music to help establish the right mood. This simple pre-activity exercise will train your state of mind to be congruent with the activity you are about to practise.

This simple idea that the patterns of your physical skill and behaviour are led by the patterns of your brain opens us up to an astonishing technique that I regard as one of the most powerful mental tools available to us: visualisation.

Visualisation – using the power of your imagination

So important is visualisation that it crops up a number of times in this book for different reasons. Visualisation is based on the premise that the mind works by using images and associations to remember the past and imagine the future. By bringing these images to mind, and the feelings associated with them, we can actually practise and refine them into our desired outcome. Whether it's performing on stage, having a tricky conversation or sliding down a mountain on ice, by imagining yourself doing it brilliantly you recruit exactly the same neural pathways in the brain that equate to actually doing that activity. With repetition, these pathways get stronger just as they would do through physical practice. The difference between physical practice and mental practice, however, is that you can do it perfectly in your mind. Therefore, you can actually enhance your ability to do something without actually having to do it.

This has huge implications in a sport such as skeleton that offers only a couple of minutes of physical training every day, but it's also essential in so many other scenarios. Have you ever wondered how a pole vaulter trains to propel themselves high into the air on the end of a bendy stick, or how a gymnast in the Cirque de Soleil plucks up the courage and confidence to perform a back flip on a high wire? Even if they have a safety net while they practise, there is still a first time for doing it without the net, and if they don't have clarity in their head (reliant on well-defined neural pathways), they will not want to attempt it.

The idea that visualised practice may actually be more effective for us than actual physical practice was tested in an NBA basketball team where the players were split into three random groups. Each group was challenged to improve their ability to score a free throw from the penalty spot over a two-week period. Group 1 were allowed to physically practise as they normally would. Group 2 could only visualise the skill over the same period, with no physical practice allowed. Group 3 were not allowed any practice. Group 2 (the visualisation group) showed the largest positive gains, followed by Group 1 (the physical group) and finally Group 3 (the no practice group). This suggests that – at least for skilled performers – there may actually be more merit to training in your head than doing it physically. There is clearly a balance to be had here, but either way it highlights a skill that I don't believe we are anywhere near utilising as well as we could.

This is just one example of some of the compelling research from the past 20 years, and now with real-time brain imagery you can back up the effects of visualisation with the observable impact it has on strengthening neural connectivity in the brain. This should make perfect sense intuitively – the better you are able to imagine doing a specific skill internally, the better your control and accuracy of that skill will be externally. Despite this, I believe that visualisation remains one of the most intuitive yet under-practised tools we have freely available to us. I'm sure that, if people understood its true power, they would do it as much as they go to the gym or brush their teeth.

Lt Luke O'Sullivan (call sign Big Muma) is an F18 fighter pilot serving with Squadron Fighter Attack 113 based in Lemoore, California. Through hard work and skilled mental aptitude, Luke has done remarkably well to get to where he is, training with the very best Top Gun instructors from the US Navy Fighter Weapons School. Needless to say, for a young fighter pilot like Luke there is a lot to learn very quickly, so the protocols of accelerated learning are as important to him as they are to our skeleton athletes.

In a jet plane capable of speeds up to Mach 1.6 (close to 2000 km/h) and g-forces spiking at 6G (similar to those experienced by skeleton athletes), it is important to first get complex skills and manoeuvres right in his head before doing them for real. Flight simulators help with this, allowing Luke to increase his hours of practice and make 'safe' mistakes, but it's visualisation that enables him to confidently translate this into the cockpit of his $100-million fighter jet. In the cockpit, pilots must apply the technical and tactical skills they have learned in the classroom. For air-to-air combat these skills are particularly demanding. Psychologically, fighter pilots must have almost superhuman capabilities of spatial and situational awareness, managing and processing complex information from various sources and making critical decisions. But, before they can do any of this, they must learn how to stay conscious. The effects of prolonged g-forces are so great that every manoeuvre becomes a fight to stop the blood draining from their brain. This induces 'grey-outs', which Luke describes as being like someone slowly drawing the curtains on your field of vision.

You can see why Luke might want to practise his flight protocols and manoeuvres in his head before taking to the skies. He and his fellow pilots normally do this sitting on a chair at the end of the pre-flight briefing – a process they simply call 'chair flying'. By this time all distractions have been removed, mobile phones especially. Luke uses the bubble technique (described earlier) to push any unhelpful thoughts or concerns outside of his bubble, leaving him space and permission to focus on key elements of the flight. 'I visualise what I am expecting to see and experience at each stage of the flight, as if I was there in the cockpit, going through the "conduct" of the mission.' Luke describes how he is seeing what he sees, hearing what he hears and feeling what he feels. He never has long before he is required to walk to the plane, but by repeating the process every day he has become exceptionally well practised.

Luke also uses visualisation not just to prime his skills but to actually get better at them. The idea here is that when you visualise something, you can isolate one skill at a time and do it perfectly – without all the distraction of everything else that may make the core skill more difficult to refine in reality. Luke can practise one manoeuvre or one component of the flight at a time in his head without the sensory overload that comes from the talking in his ear, the hundreds of dials and lights in the cockpit, or the need to withstand the g-forces. Together these could all be overwhelming; in isolation they can be carefully honed. This allows him to layer one skill at a time without compromising the quality of each layer. It is visualisation that makes the process possible where in the real situation it might not be.

Taking the same principle, a study at Stanford University found that, when visualisation was introduced to gymnasts' training routines, it allowed them to successfully master complex, multi-layered routines which up to that point they hadn't been successful at.

The likes of gymnasts, fighter pilots, free solo climbers and surgeons all have one thing in common: none of them will accept a trial-and-error approach to getting better – they can't. With all the simulations and safety nets in the world, they simply don't want to practise getting it wrong more than they have to. They may be brave and highly skilled people, but every mistake has the potential to undermine their confidence. Visualisation becomes their friend in learning.

Using visualisation to enhance a skill

Identify something simple you would like to improve or do well at. It could be a new skill you are learning or an existing skill you want to perfect. Visualisation to enhance a skill is best done in intense 10-minute bursts, including time to get into the right state of mind to do it properly.

Start by taking 10 deep and relaxing breaths. You should only ever visualise in a state of mind that best suits the skill you are practising. If you are tense in the body or busy in the mind, you will not be teaching your brain the right cues.

Visualisation is as much about what you feel as what you see. Practise using all your senses. Notice what you see, feel, hear and smell around you, immersing yourself in the environment in which you will be. You should NOT be watching yourself from the outside as if you were on TV, instead you are looking out through your own eyes and feeling what you feel. Identify specific cues that help you to stay focused on the process. For example, if you are delivering a speech, it may be a combination of posture, breathing and delivering key messages in a confident manner. Stay focused on them.

Whatever you visualise, keep it accurate and positive – it's better to imagine a few simple skills done perfectly with a break in between than a whole performance done averagely. Keep it steady. We tend to rush in our mind, especially if the activity we are visualising makes us feel slightly nervous. This can be the source of many errors, so, if this is the case, take a deep breath and slow everything down as you breathe out. If you need to, you can even 'press pause' on what's going on around you while you regain composure – that's the beauty of visualisation.

If you struggle to visualise at first, don't worry. Try these tips:

- Do it little and often. The more you practise, the better you will get.
- Keep it simple. Visualisation takes a surprising amount of focus and mental energy when done properly, so break it down into small chunks and put them together over time.
- If you find yourself imagining mistakes or inaccuracies, try reverse-visualisation. This is when you practise things you have just done well in real life. If you've just had a positive experience, going back over it in your head will help reinforce the positive associations of that skill, making you more likely to repeat it consistently well in the future. You are simply encouraging the repetition of 'good' in your mind.

Visualisation isn't just about enhancing physical skills; it can also prepare you emotionally and intellectually for challenging events, raising the bar on your ability to manage difficult and complex situations, as well as helping you to maintain composure and confidence under pressure. These specific variations we will cover further on, but for now let's look at how you can develop some complementary mental skills.

9
Connections: build your mental blueprint

Repetition is an essential part of the accelerated learning equation, but clearly it's not enough. In fact, there is a danger that mindless practice could interfere with your learning and even make you worse. Evidence would suggest that, up to a point, you will get better at something by simply doing it, even if you are relatively aimless in the act. But eventually there comes a level of expertise where you must strive to narrow down the pathways of excellence.

Imagine chiselling away at a huge chunk of marble with the intent of shaping a beautiful statue. At first it's probably okay to knock off large chunks as you hone in on the general shape and size. But as you get closer to its final form you need to start being far more selective, careful, focused and patient. The tools you use become far more refined and you begin to pay more attention to small details. In much the same way, you are trying to shape and refine the pathways of your brain to exact the skills and behaviours that allow you to succeed at the highest level.

This is not just analogous of how pathways in the brain become more and more refined in line with the quality of your 'technique'; it's also a good metaphor for the lived experience of going through such a process. We can all relate to how much fun it must be to smash away at a marble rock with hammer and chisel, and maybe it's this sense of fun that brings the motivation to keep coming back in the initial stages of the project. But by the time you have to start paying attention to tiny details, you might have a very different relationship with the project. Fun is still important (as you will see when we talk about resonance later) but it will inevitably be a different kind of fun.

In the same way, an entrepreneur with their own exciting start-up business may make big chunks of visible progress as they embark upon a new venture, fuelled by the excitement that comes from doing quite literally anything. From product development to branding, marketing to sales, almost every activity translates into progress when you start from ground zero. But as the venture moves further along, the shape of the business evolves and refines simultaneously, requiring much more strategic attention and finessing.

For me this is the most important of our principles of mental aptitude for one simple reason: if you form the wrong connections in the first place, then not only do you create unwanted habits and learn incorrect technique but you will also have to spend considerable time and energy unlearning these in order to progress beyond that point.

Tip for coaches

Making the right connections must be an active process driven by the athlete and supported by the coach, not a passive process for the athlete driven by the coach. If your goal is to organise and strengthen your mental process in order that you are more consistent and confident in your own mind, then you cannot have someone else do all the thinking for you. When an athlete is on the start line at the Olympics, the only voice they have inside their head is their own. Confidence in their own mind is everything. If the coach gives too much instruction because they want to 'save' the athletes from making mistakes, then they may be helping them in that moment but are bypassing the opportunity for the athlete to make and strengthen that connection themselves. From a mental development perspective, the job of the coach is to support the athletes in correcting themselves. This is a subtle but profound difference.

Our relationship with goals

The difference between *being busy* and *making progress* boils down to your ability to internalise clear goals. It is these that give you direction.

There is a universal truth that rings true for all industries – the consistently high achievement of teams and individuals doesn't happen by accident. No one can achieve success simply by turning up and seeing what happens. You certainly wouldn't want your surgeon to do that if you were having an operation, and neither would your team want you to do it. Of course, the more skill and experience you have, the more you might be able to avoid planning and preparation, but if success is built upon consistency, then hoping for the best is not going to work.

Despite the unquestionable merits of setting goals as a means of making meaningful progress, I often notice a lot of resistance when it comes to mapping out clear goals. I suspect this is because goals can be scary – once you've set a goal, you've created the conditions in which success or failure become real. This in turn can induce stress because your goals require you to learn things you don't yet know, set standards, be disciplined and productive, and challenge the limits of your ability. But this stress shouldn't be seen as a bad thing. It's this challenge that creates the intensity you need to be more focused and committed to every step along the way. The heightened sense of challenge and intensity that comes about through setting clear goals cannot, and should not, be avoided.

You often notice when people are shying away from the real challenge of goals because they define them too broadly. In doing so, you ignore the myriad of smaller challenges that sit underneath it. This is great for peace of mind, but rubbish for actually achieving it or getting better. Phrases like 'we need to improve our diversity in the business' roll easily off the tongue if you don't have to do anything about diversity. A simple label can make a complex problem go away, but it can obscure complexity so much that you lose sight of it. And that can come as a great relief.

I spend a significant amount of time turning unclear goals into clear ones – both for myself and in helping others. By doing this, you often discover a multifaceted problem consisting of many parts. All of these parts play differently to your strengths, weaknesses, insecurities and confidence. The only thing to do at this point is to separate them out into their own discrete challenges and goals. This way, goal setting becomes less about articulating a nice clear outcome in one neat sentence (as is the focus of SMART goals, which stands for Specific, Measurable, Attainable, Realistic, Timely). Rather, it's about having a network of interlinking goals that all feed off one another. Importantly, this is exactly how the brain works, using neural connections to create patterns and associations from one thing to another, allowing us to see the world as a whole system rather than as millions of individual entities (which would be chaotic and confusing). This interconnection of goals becomes our 'mental blueprint' for success, enabling us to visualise our goals as a dynamic map rather than just a static end-point. I will share an example of this in the next section and using Figure 9.1.

Understanding the principles that sit behind *why* you do things allows you to focus on what really matters, while letting go of the noise – the things that just aren't important. This is arguably one of the greatest skills of high-performing teams. My experience with British skeleton was a great example of this. I remember the first couple of weeks I spent with the team, which was really about observation and seeking to understand the demands of the sport. Having observed the team and got to know their individual habits and routines, I played back to them what I had noticed and asked them why they did certain things in a particular way. The most common responses I got? 'Because I've always done it like that.' 'Because my coach has told me to do it like that.' 'Because the world champion does it like that, and if it's good enough for them, it's good enough for me.' At face value, all legitimate reasons, but none of these responses demonstrates an understanding of how it actually makes them better at the sport, how it contributes towards their system for getting the best out of themselves.

Another good example of this is the US women's football team, who for years have been pretty much unbeatable in the sport. Unshackled by convention (which in Europe has been forged by the men's game over many decades), the American women started with a blank piece of paper and asked the simple question: 'How do we get good at this?' Consequently, they have taken a very different approach to recruiting and developing their players, and have adopted the latest advances in sport science far more readily than their European counterparts. During the 2019 Women's World Cup I heard one of the commentators remark, 'It's amazing how well the Americans do, considering they don't play any of their football in Europe.' I couldn't help but ponder the irony of this statement. Surely, it's *because* they don't play in Europe – they haven't been restricted by unhelpful conventions and therefore are able to think and play differently.

Goal setting in this way helps you to make the most of your limited energy by helping you to challenge the very nature of what you do and why you do it. This is the reason why goal setting is nearly always one of the first conversations I have with a client. Here are some example questions I find useful to have up my sleeve:

- What exactly would you like to achieve or aim for?
- Why is achieving this so important to you as a person?
- How effective are you being in how you get there?
- What makes the biggest difference towards achieving this goal?
- What do you find yourself doing in a certain way because you've always done it that way?
- What are you not doing that you know you should be?
- What have you learned from experience that might help you?
- How and when do you apply this experience in order to keep moving forward?

These have the potential to be quite challenging questions, but they further highlight the importance of being able to clarify the goal along with its discrete challenges.

Designing your mental blueprint

Becoming the architect of your own mind requires you to design a mental blueprint. The mental blueprint is effectively a mind map for success. It breaks down big goals and aspirations into discrete areas of performance and then further into everyday habits, routines, skills and techniques. This is a much more dynamic way of goal setting than simply defining your outcome in one neat sentence. It maps out how one goal relates to another, which adds meaning and purpose to the fabric of everything you do.

These mental blueprints became essential to the athletes and coaches on the British skeleton team. It was effectively a plan on a page for achieving success – whatever 'success' meant to each individual. It also helped them to live and breathe an Inside-Out mindset by reminding them of how much they could control. Figure 9.1 shows a slightly watered-down example of this.

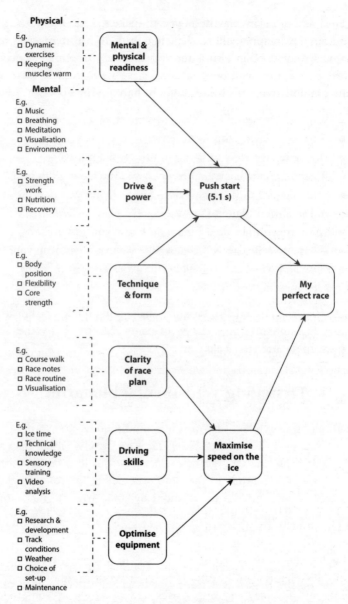

FIGURE 9.1 Example of a goal-setting tree used in skeleton

The idea of calling it a 'blueprint' was not just about internal branding. It was very deliberate. A blueprint isn't just a vision for what you want to build – it's a detailed intent. By having a blueprint for the perfect race, you create a consistent vision to strive towards. Many times I have been challenged on using the word 'perfect'. It sits uncomfortably with some people and I understand why. So let me explain what I mean.

The blueprint ultimately links to visualisation and how you see yourself performing. For any given scenario we all have an expectation – for example, 'I have to stand up on stage and deliver a presentation to 100 people'. At this point the goal is rather vague and focused more on the output than the input. So what happens when you start to add more details? How do you want to address them? What do you want to wear? What do you want to say exactly? How will you stay calm and relaxed? How long will you give yourself? How will you use the space? So now you have the makings of a blueprint, all that's left is to imagine what good will look like in each of these areas. But do you want to visualise good – maybe with the occasional stumble and slightly less impact – or do you want to visualise perfect?

You see, I think we actually put more undue pressure on ourselves by *not* being able to imagine what perfect looks and feels like – even if we never achieve it in reality.

When it comes to mental imagery, anything other than perfect creates room for ambiguity and doubt. In exactly the same way, the blueprints for a building represent the exact dimensions and characteristics for that building, but when the building gets built, is it perfect? Not in the true sense – there will be small inconsistencies that naturally come about through either human error or working with raw materials. But does this mean there is no point in having the blueprint in the first place? No, absolutely not. If the blueprint didn't exist, then the whole project would be full of inconsistencies and vulnerable to gross errors.

In the skeleton team I heard the same nervousness about creating a blueprint. The key to using it was understanding the difference between expectance and acceptance. It's more compelling to work towards a well-defined blueprint with the acceptance that things do not always go perfectly than to work towards a poorly defined goal with an expectation of achieving it.

You might argue that this philosophy is far easier to live by when the activity you are trying to be world class at is relatively contained and without too many elements outside of your control. In the army we had the motto, 'No plan survives contact with the enemy.' Boxer Mike Tyson put it just as eloquently: 'Everybody has a plan until they get punched in the mouth.' But that's not the same as saying, 'Don't bother with a plan.' I can't speak for Tyson, but certainly in the military, planning is key to adapting.

Throughout his career World Cup-winning rugby player Jonny Wilkinson had a clearly defined vision of the perfect game of rugby, not because he ever expected to play it but because it was an essential reference point for how well he responded to familiar scenarios and how he executed his skills. In doing so, it helped him to respond positively to mistakes as well as the inevitable twists and turns of the game.

Quieten your inner critic

There is another important role of the mental blueprint. Each of the skeleton athletes typically started their blueprint of the perfect race by breaking down the race into the push start at the top of the track and then maximising their speed on ice. Then they would break down their perfect push start into smaller areas of focus until they got to the granular detail – take a deep, relaxing breath, place the sled into the grooves of the track, drive off with the back leg, and so on.

Once you get down to this level of detail, you don't leave any room for ambiguity. You simply need to focus on the routine, one step at a time. By understanding how you have arrived at this point, you can let go of the workings-out and focus on the quality of your routine. This gives you the confidence you need – thinking clearly and positively.

This helps to answer a concern I hear a lot when it comes to mental training. Is there a danger that we overthink what we are doing? The overthinkers reading this will understand immediately the perils of this. Trying to process so much information, the brain is unable to focus on anything. It can be disorienting and paralysing for many people. If this is you, then you would be forgiven for not wanting to try any exercises that encourage you to think any more. But this is the point. You need to do the thinking upfront so that you don't have to do it at the point of performance, when all you should be focusing on is doing.

If you haven't done your homework, it leaves you vulnerable to your inner voice and critic. 'Are you sure about this?' 'Is this the right thing to be doing?' 'What are other people doing?' 'If you get this wrong, you're going to look stupid.'

Never is this principle more important than when you are under pressure to get results. As we discovered earlier, when you are under pressure your mind is much more susceptible to anxiety and negative thinking.

In the absence of a plan to maintain focus it's more likely that clear thinking will give way to fear or panic. The simple act of planning can prime the brain to stay focused. Planning while in a calm and rational state of mind helps you to prioritise your attention and do all the difficult calculations upfront so that you don't have to when you're under pressure.

Staying focused on your own race

If your blueprint is an intellectual process, then the reality of executing the blueprint is very much a lived experience. If the blueprint represents the instructions for being at your best, you still need to follow the instructions. This is easier said than done, as anyone who has tried building flatpack furniture will testify. If you think you know best and decide to freestyle it, you run the risk of getting it wrong and having to start again (as I am all too aware).

In the world of athletics, there is no greater reason to ignore the instructions than the sight of other people racing ahead of you. And there is no better example of the mental blueprint at work than Kelly Holmes' performance to win the women's 800 metres Olympic gold at the 2004 Athens Games. After the first lap Kelly found herself in last place. Many people assumed this was her intent because that's all they could see. Watching the race unfurl, it would be easy to think that she deliberately placed herself at the back in order to then move forward through the order. In reality, she was trying to be neither at the back nor at the front – she was simply focusing on running her own perfect race.

One of the BBC commentators that night, Brendan Foster, suggested that the victory was down to consistent pacing. Kelly's times for each lap were exactly the same – 58.2 seconds precisely – suggesting to me that she had a plan in her head that wasn't governed by what the others were doing. Her plan was governed by the internal blueprint of what the perfect race should feel like. She was racing her perfect race. The fact that other competitors ran off quickly at the beginning was neither here nor there. Kelly stuck to her blueprint, which takes a huge amount of discipline, trust and focus.

This is exactly the same sentiment that many traders and hedge fund managers in the money markets talk about. Successful financial trader Martin Burton once explained that the most important thing for any trader is to focus on their own system regardless of what the market is doing. Traders who abandon their own method to chase the market can expect only one thing: consistent losses coupled with the odd success. Those who stay focused on their plan will enjoy consistent success coupled with the odd loss.

In reality, following your own plan is as much an emotional process as it is an intellectual one. Therefore in Chapter 11 we explore the role of emotions in being at our best.

10
Feedback: make more of every experience

Feedback has been the hot topic of many a leadership book and training course. And for good reason – it's an essential part of the learning process. Having arrived at the end of an important project or competition, it's easy to collapse in a heap and thank God that you've made it to the end. But for elite performers and teams, the project isn't over. Having invested so much time and effort in getting this far, you need to be able to go back and join the dots in order to take anything meaningful from the experience. In this way, a consistent and quality feedback process is like compound interest over time. Success is built upon the accumulation of small learning opportunities. By taking these opportunities you build upon past gains – creating exponential growth in your capacity to learn and get better.

When I compare my experiences across business, sport and the military, I'm not sure there's a single word that evokes such a different range of thoughts and emotions as the word 'feedback'. Being honest, it's definitely business that is behind the curve on this one, where feedback is a proxy for someone telling you what they think of you. It's just not valued in quite the same way as it seems to be in the military and sport – no sooner is one project or deal completed than all eyes are on the next one: 'time is money'. This is a falsehood, and there is no better way to stunt growth and improvement than pandering to the next opportunity before adapting from the last. Done well, however, feedback doesn't have to be a chore or take that long. With the right process in place it can be a welcome chance to step back and reflect while celebrating progress and seeking new opportunity.

This is a mindset as much as anything. Feedback needs to come from a genuine curiosity to understand what just happened. Almost always there is a technical lesson and a psychological lesson to learn. Did you lose concentration? Were you fully committed? Overconfident? Impatient? Psyched out by other people? Tired?

It's only by understanding these dynamics that every loss is an opportunity for growth. Only through this process will you become more psychologically astute and sensitive to good and bad practice.

In environments where there's a shared understanding that we are here to get better, anything that will allow us to move closer to our mission is fervently encouraged. This is made much easier when the mission is clearly defined and when the feedback has some structure to it.

This may be a good time to return to Luke, our fighter pilot serving with Squadron Fighter Attack 113 in California. When reflecting on the feedback process, one of the observations Luke made was that the further you get as a fighter pilot, the more you realise how little you know. When you're surrounded by Top Gun instructors, knowledge and experience are in abundance, but there are set protocols for how these are dispensed. The time for feedback is in the debrief sessions after every flight, and this time is sacred. Luke confidently states that this is where 95 per cent of his learning occurs – not in the sky but in the briefing room. What happens in the sky creates the opportunity to learn lessons, but this opportunity has not been converted into lessons until it has been through the briefing room.

A 'low-key' debrief will take as long as the flight itself, but a more complex debrief will take significantly longer. This is because the debrief actually runs multiple times, each time focusing on a different element of performance, for example communication, tactics or manoeuvres. For communication, for instance, they will focus solely on the correct use of voice procedure and protocol, reinforcing good practice and correcting bad. Every pilot has a chance to correct their mistakes first, but if they miss anything then another pilot can make the correction. Out of pride they like to avoid this happening – but ego never gets in the way of learning. On occasions, the elite Top Gun pilots will be corrected by their more junior and less experienced counterparts. They are surprisingly encouraging of this when it happens – they don't often make mistakes so it's a genuine opportunity to learn when they do. They also want to see other pilots doing well – all ships rise in a high tide. In addition, all feedback is depersonalised – the goal is not to shame you so they never use your name; they use your plane's call sign instead.

Perhaps most surprisingly, pilots are given two hours between landing the aircraft on deck and the start of the debrief, in order to give them time to prepare individually. This ensures that they are able to maximise the quality of learning during the session. In fact, one of the key performance indicators pilots are assessed on is their contribution to the debrief.

This all demonstrates how instrumental feedback is when the goal is to be the very best.

Total recall

Given that this is a book about personal leadership, I want to highlight a particular source of feedback that we all get, every day. I am talking about the feedback we give ourselves. I am always curious as to why so many training courses focus on the feedback we give or we receive from other people (still extremely important) without addressing the feedback that is going on inside our own head nearly all the time. If this feedback is poor (maybe we're focusing disproportionately on the mistakes we make), then imagine what it does to the system.

In the section about identity we learned that, by measuring 'avoidance' and 'approach' activity in the brain, we need to respect ourselves in order to respond positively to the challenge of a difficult, ambiguous or volatile situation. In essence, those with high self-esteem were able to deal better with challenge and ambiguity. That's worth remembering here because it stands to reason that the quality of feedback we give ourselves will be hugely affected by what we think about ourselves. If we don't believe we are capable or worthy of success, then we will be primed to look for the evidence to back this belief up, for example 'That person ignored me because I'm not worth listening to' or 'I didn't get selected for the team because I'm not good enough.' It is this internal feedback that we need to get right first and foremost, so I want to share with you some ways in which you can ensure the feedback you give yourself is accurate, honest and compassionate.

Our memory recall is an essential component of the feedback we are able to generate for ourselves. It's one thing to be good at analysing our performance and to make accurate sense of what just happened, but this assumes that we are remembering the right things in the first place. There's a charming saying in the army which is rather apt here: 'Shit in, shit out.' The quality of analysis means nothing if the data we are analysing is flawed. In the same way, it doesn't matter how clever and technologically advanced your satellite navigation system is – if you put the wrong data into it, you will end up in the wrong place.

Back in the skeleton team, this posed both a challenge and an opportunity. If an athlete gets to the bottom of the mountain, looks up and says, 'What just happened?' they have effectively lost half a day's training. That's not entirely true as they will have video footage for some of the corners; however, this is limited if they don't have an internal reference point to compare it to.

When you first go down the ice, the whole experience is such a sensory overload that it leaves little processing power for remembering or analysing anything in any detail. When athletes are new to the sport, their first challenge is to simply count how many corners they went round, and most even get that wrong (as I did when I tried it at half the speed). Therefore part of our ability to accurately recall previous experiences relies upon us being in a controlled physiological state throughout the process – which happens to be a key component of Part 2 of this book, 'The Feeling Dimension'.

To improve our capacity for accurate recall we applied a number of other training principles. First, time. The sooner the athlete is able to reverse-visualise (go back over the run in their mind), the richer the information they will recall. Sounds obvious, but practicalities can easily get in the way of this. In this case there was a bus sitting at the bottom of the mountain with a queue of other athletes waiting to be driven back up the mountain so that they could talk to their coaches. On the trip back up the mountain, the memory trace was getting weaker and athletes started to dwell on mistakes they had made. All of this led to considerable memory distortion.

A few very small changes to this routine had a significant effect on enhancing recall and with it the speed of learning and confidence. Instead of waiting to get back up to the top of the mountain and relying on their coach to offer feedback, athletes would finish their run and head straight to a designated space where they would have their notebooks, pen and a radio for communication. No one was allowed to talk to the athlete until they were ready. Their first action was to go back through the run in their head making any notes as appropriate.

Some athletes had much better recall than others, and, unsurprisingly, this was directly correlated with their speed of learning and adoption of new techniques. Over time every athlete got better at memory recall simply by adopting this process. Linked to the principles of neuroscience, most important was that they were in the right state of mind to recall their run as clearly as possible. Encouragingly, they could see themselves getting better as their recall started to match more closely with their video footage. If you make the mistake of watching the video footage first, then your recall will be shaped by what you see on the screen and you won't ever learn to give yourself more accurate internal feedback.

Joining the dots – left page–right page technique

In the same way, it's important for the athletes to have a habitual process for analysing not just what happened but also how well they achieved their predetermined goals. This is a thought process that can be trained by using a simple methodology I developed called 'left page–right page'. In their notebook they use the left-hand pages to write down their intentions (feed-forward) and the right-hand page to write down what actually happened (feedback).

Left page (feed-forward)

On the left-hand page athletes would write between two and four goals for their training session. It could have been a technical goal like 'Steer high in corner 5, maintaining pressure on the exit' or a more sensory goal such as 'Focus on deep breathing and relaxation in the final five minutes prior to my run'. Typically, they would have done this after video analysis the day before, so their goals were progressive and linked to previous feedback.

Right page (feedback)

The right page they would complete straight after the run, having reverse-visualised the run in their head. They would focus only on the goals they had set themselves on the left page and measure themselves against how well they had executed those goals. This tended to be a mark out of 10 with a short description. If there was anything outside the remit of these left-page goals that needed examination, they could do that only after addressing the priority left-page goals.

Despite all the technical details, success should only ever be defined by one simple question: 'Did I do what I said I was going to do?' If the answer to this question is 'yes', then you have succeeded in the truest sense, regardless of the result. You cannot ask more of anyone who did what they said they were going to do. If you adopt this philosophy in your own business, you'll find it's amazing how it starts to focus people on the quality of feed-forward.

I have always made a pact with my clients that the only failure is not doing what we agreed to do – which places the emphasis on how we set ourselves up for success in the first place. This idea echoes in so many high performers – by focusing on the quality of their preparation and mental work upfront, they are still able to perceive a loss as a success so long as they did what they planned to do.

In addition to using these day-to-day training protocols to enhance internal feedback and therefore learning, many athletes promote the benefit of meditation as part of their daily practice. The benefits of meditation are well documented for having a profound effect on mental performance. By measuring the electrical activity of the brain using an electroencephalogram (EEG), scientists have demonstrated how people well practised at meditation exhibit profound changes in gamma activity compared to novices.[1] This type of brainwave activity encourages large-scale coordination across different areas of the brain leading to a more stable and coherent mental experience. The consequences of this are significant for maximising our attentional control, processing speed, intuition and learning ability. We will look more at applied meditation in the Feeling Dimension.

With this combination of simple techniques used over a prolonged period of time, we are all capable of conditioning our performance considerably. This leaves one final but important topic for the Thinking Dimension: using emotions to accelerate our learning.

11

Resonance: turn a downward spiral into an upward spiral

Whether you like it or not, emotions play an essential role in how you think, learn and perform. As a quick thought experiment, how many times do you have to touch a hot iron in order to learn the lesson 'never touch a hot iron'? Once, maybe twice if you're a slow learner! This is a simple illustration of a fundamental principle: the strength of emotion that accompanies an experience has a significant impact on what you take from that experience. For example, the emotional spike you get from burning your hand adds 'resonance' to the experience of reaching out for a hot iron, accelerating the learning process. Typically, we associate this effect with bad experiences thanks to our negative bias towards survival, which we spoke about earlier. It's no wonder we become preoccupied with 'not making mistakes', a very limiting mode of psychology. This makes downward spirals (situations where one negative thought or action leads to another) very common in competitive environments.

But what if you could apply the same principle to positive experiences – thereby creating an upward spiral? I don't mean ignoring mistakes or things done badly, I simply mean predisposing yourself to focus on what you *can* do rather than what you *can't* do. For a brain designed around survival, this doesn't come naturally; instead you have to condition yourself to this way of thinking. In order to do this you must be more deliberate in how you combine your thoughts and emotions – especially when you are analysing your performance. Therefore in this section we will look at techniques for using emotions to actually enhance your performance rather than limit it. But first it would be helpful to know how resonance works in the brain.

As you already know, every time a neural pathway fires in the brain, that pathway is strengthened, meaning that less energy is required to activate the pathway in the future. This is one of the key principles of neuroplasticity – our ability to learn, change and adapt. But this strengthening process isn't just influenced by repetition; it is also influenced by resonance – the strength of electrical charge sent down the neural pathway. The greater the emotional significance of an event, the greater the resonance and the faster the pathway is strengthened.

This is the neurological basis of why we retain more information about events that have emotional significance for us. This is the basis of inspiration, motivation and pride, all essential ingredients in the recipe for achieving your greatest goals.

Working with your emotions, not against them

It is easy to think that people who consistently perform at the highest level are robots. At least from the outside they never seem to have a bad day; instead they remain disciplined, routined and focused. But their ability to be these things is really only part of the performance equation – emotions still play a huge role in their inner world. In my work with elite athletes, soldiers, musicians and business leaders, they generally all experience the full suite of emotions like the rest of us – disappointment, fear, frustration, anger, pride, satisfaction, excitement and so on. The difference is how they put these emotions to work.

Broadly, we have two ways of dealing with emotions – we can suppress them or reappraise them (work with them). This was brilliantly illustrated in a study where volunteers watched gruesome videos of animal slaughter and human surgery.[1] Some were asked to suppress their emotional responses by deliberately not showing any disgust in their expression – this group were the 'suppressers'. Others were asked to adopt the stance of a professional while watching the videos, by focusing on the technique of the surgeon, for example, as if they were going to be asked to carry out the procedure in the future. This group were the 'reappraisers'.

Both groups reported that they felt less emotion when compared with a control group who just watched the films, but there the similarities ended. In the reappraisal group, the frontal lobes of the rational brain showed a surge of activity a few seconds after the video began (indicating thoughtfulness and focus), while at the same time the limbic system (emotional brain) reduced in activity. By 'leaning in' and making sense of what was happening the 'reappraisers' were able to stay effective in the face of potential emotional distress. In the 'suppressers' group, meanwhile, activity in the limbic system increased significantly. It would seem that by showing outward denial of what is happening (leaning away), you are actually stoking the emotional fire further.

Suppressing emotions without reappraising them increases adrenaline-linked arousal responses, including raised heart rate, blood pressure and skin sweatiness. It also lessens your memory of an event. Reappraising, however, doesn't make the same sort of constant demands on the brain as suppression does. It's why language such as 'staying on top of our emotions' isn't always helpful.

Suppression has other costs, too. It is rather a blunt instrument, and because emotions such as fear, sexual arousal and anger have so many overlapping 'symptoms', suppressing a negative emotion almost inevitably leads to the suppression of other positive emotions. In high-performance environments this is problematic because positive emotions are essential to the way you experience reward and satisfaction, and therefore your ability to build confidence and learn faster. In addition, people whose style it is to suppress emotions rather than reappraise them don't share their emotions with other people nearly as much as reappraisers do. They are therefore less likely to seek help and support and are, on average, less well liked by other people. This is because we tend to trust and like people who are open and self-disclosing.

These findings challenge many preconceptions about what it means to be emotionally resilient. They also suggest you can absolutely use dominant emotions like anger, but only with great care and to a clear purpose.

Using visualisation to train emotional control

I have already introduced the concept of visualisation. We specifically spoke about it as a tool for rehearsing skills and techniques, but it is also an essential tool for developing our desired emotional response to a meaningful situation.

A great example of this comes from the world of financial traders. The essence of making money on the stock market is about making rational decisions based on the likelihood of stocks going up or down. As with any other performance, the success of traders relies upon having a mental blueprint to guide their rational process – this is known as a 'trading plan'. By having a clear rationale for when they buy a stock and when they sell a stock, they should be able to factor for any unexpected moves in the market, thereby allowing them to manage risk. But, just like any performance athlete, they too are susceptible to emotions when markets rise and fall suddenly, and these emotions distort how well they adhere to their plan.

Importantly, the best traders tend to recognise emotions as part of the 'experience' of trading, choosing to work with them rather than deny them or fight them. Interestingly, this defensive denial of emotions is something that has been shown to be more prevalent in younger, less experienced traders.

Visualisation becomes a great tool for helping traders work with their emotions and maintain clarity of thought in chaotic market conditions, or when they have multiple trades open at the same time. Using the trading plan to play out various scenarios, good traders ask themselves: 'When the price is at a different level from where I want it to be, how am I going to be feeling, what am I likely to be thinking and what will I be doing? Am I a buyer or a seller at that level? I know I will have to be one or the other. Once I have worked this out and tested myself against my own level of pain, then I can proceed, knowing that if the price ends up there I will be familiar enough with the emotion to make the right call.'

This form of mental preparation is a natural extension to your blueprint and helps you to prepare for the full range of emotions you may experience in different scenarios. As demonstrated in this example, emotional planning is a critical tool if you wish to control your mind when you arrive at an important juncture. We will look at this further in the Feeling Dimension when we explore expanding your comfort zone.

Emotional 'charging'

So how else can you work with emotions to create an upward spiral rather than a downward spiral? The answer to that can be found on the ski slopes of the Alps, the playground for one of the most skilful and daring athletes I have worked with – a freestyle mogul skier.

As if skiing over moguls isn't hard enough, freestyle moguls include ramps at regular intervals down the course from which skiers launch into the air and perform aerial stunts of varying difficulty. The moment they land they are straight back into the punishing moguls, their legs working like shock absorbers and their hips twisting left and right at unbelievable speeds. Athletes are measured both for their speed down the course and their air (jumps). Freestyle mogul skiing is a unique mix of brutal physicality with creative flair. With their bodies running high on a cocktail of adrenaline, endorphins and dopamine, their response at the bottom is very often one of either total jubilation or total desolation, dependent almost entirely on whether they landed their jumps or not. There's very little in between.

I soon noticed that when athletes land a good routine they would want to go and share it straight away with teammates, coaches and fellow competitors, but if they didn't, they would want to be on their own, ruminating on what they did wrong. Over many repetitions, this has a marked effect on how the brain is processing and learning from experience. By dwelling on mistakes while experiencing negative emotions such as disappointment and regret, it charges and reinforces these negative pathways in the brain. Conversely, when an athlete nailed their routine, they would be less inclined to review and reinforce what went well. This is analogous to how we all deal with success and failure, but with a little pre-thought you can put these positive emotions to better use.

The first ingredient for doing this is making feedback specific. Raw emotions are fairly unhelpful to us unless they can be channelled into specific lessons or actions. Think about how you would react to the following two statements.

Well done, you did an amazing job today.

Sounds good, right? We would all like more of that in our lives. But how useful is it really? It will probably give you a warm, fuzzy glow for a little while, but once this has worn off, what does it leave you with?

How about this statement?

> Well done in your presentation today. Your eye contact with the audience was excellent and it made them feel really engaged. Your arguments were also exceptionally clear and compelling. It was definitely worth the time you spent preparing.

Here, the same feeling of pride and satisfaction gets channelled into very clear pathways for success and you can guarantee that next time you are doing a presentation you will want to do the following things well:

- Give the audience eye contact.
- Make your arguments clear and compelling.
- Spend time preparing.

By taking the time to compile this feedback, you have applied resonance to specific behavioural pathways in the brain, and, just as with the hot iron, you have accelerated their development. Therefore the feedback you give yourself should be defined less by whether it is 'good' or 'bad' and more by whether it helps you to channel your effort. Put simply, it must be as specific as possible. I have to confess, it took me a while to write that second statement because it's hard work making feedback specific! But with effective feed-forward (using the left-page–right page technique), feedback should be one of the easiest parts of the Thinking Dimension.

This is a principle that I had the opportunity to apply with positive effect with the executive team of a large independent retailer in Ireland. I've always really enjoyed working with retail teams, I think because it's very close to working in sport. The environment is extremely results-driven and competitive. Sales are easily and quickly measured, therefore every decision about every product on the shelf is quantifiable and easy to test. The figures speak for themselves, which inevitably creates winners and losers. Managers take advantage of this by constantly setting new targets for their teams to beat in an attempt to spur them on and sell more. When targets are hit and competitors are beaten, there's a palpable sense of reward and satisfaction. Until the next target is set.

In this fast-paced environment, emotions can run rampant through the corridors of power. Technology now allows information to pass from till to CEO almost instantaneously – revenue per hour, percentage gains and losses year-on-year, stock count, average spend per customer, the list goes on. Each member of the senior team is drip-fed a constant stream of data coming through on their mobile phones. Without the appropriate discipline, they can easily turn into results junkies, allowing their emotions to be dictated by the numbers. These are the kinds of techniques used in psychology labs to induce 'learned helplessness', a condition in which, rather than controlling the situation, you allow the situation to control you. In the case of this particular business, the Outside-In effect was being exacerbated by the wider economic downturn and a global shift in how consumers purchased their goods, moving from high street to online.

It was in the Monday morning executive team meetings that we decided to target this particular downward spiral. What had been happening was that the team would start off by discussing results from the previous week – good or bad. Departments wanted to know how they ranked and therefore how they were 'performing'. Very often, this led to a conversation about needing to do better, after which they would set targets for the upcoming period ... and so the cycle continued. Staff on the shop floor would wait in anticipation to see what version of their manager would return from the weekly update. As the business struggled more and more, this created a downward spiral that was difficult to break free from. Morale was affecting performance on the shop floor, and the performance on the shop floor was affecting morale.

In order to break this cycle, our first step was to ban any data from the Monday morning meeting until such time as the cycle had been reversed. Instead, it was all about defining intent – feed-forward. Each department head would decide exactly where they wanted to apply their attention and the specific controllable goals they would go after in the upcoming few weeks. It was essential to get strong traction in a small number of areas rather than trying to control everything – they all needed to feel a victory on some level.

The next Monday, sales figures were kept off the table and instead each member of the team had to remind the others what they had committed to the week before. The question was simply: Have you done what you said you were going to do? What impact is it having? What feedback can you offer each other to help bolster this effort? 'Left-page' goals were renewed before they went about the new week, again focusing on intent rather than outcomes.

As the weeks went on, small victories started to build. Negativity and reactivity gave way to positivity and proactivity. Positive emotions gave them the opportunity to dig into these victories, to amplify their resonance but also to reinforce specific actions and behaviours that were working. As competitive as each department was, the victories were shared – 'all ships rise in a high tide'. Before long, the sales data was reintroduced into the equation, but only if the outputs could be connected to clear inputs from the previous week.

Remarkably, by bringing the team together around victories rather than defeats, they started to communicate far more openly with one another, they demonstrated more compassion and patience with their staff, and they gave each other much more encouragement and positive feedback. This lifted the shop floor, giving everyone permission to focus on day-to-day deliverables without worrying about outcomes they couldn't control. Less reliant on the output data to tell them whether they were doing a good job, they became far more intuitive around the inputs – leading to one of their most successful years in recent history.

The message here is very simple and translates to all performance environments: don't let success go to waste. This is about more than simply celebrating success – it's about understanding it and reinforcing it. Only by doing this can you create upward spirals.

In the next part of the book, we explore the Feeling Dimension and the incredible interaction between your psychology and our physiology (mind and body). Here we expand on the role that emotions play in our search for peak performance, we explore the limits of our ability as well as how to cope with periods of prolonged intensity. You will learn how to recondition your body's response to challenge and, with it, how to expand your comfort zone.

PART 2

The Feeling Dimension

'Nothing great was ever achieved without enthusiasm.'

Ralph Waldo Emerson

Section 3: The mind–body connection

12

Intensity: keeping it together when the stakes are high

Dropped into the night sky over hostile territory or diving through the murky darkness of the sea towards an enemy vessel, in the moments before 'contact' there is calm contemplation. Special Forces soldiers must out-think as well as outmanoeuvre their adversaries – often at times when they are already physically depleted.

UK Special Forces are predominantly made up of two units – the Special Air Service (SAS) and the Special Boat Service (SBS). They are most effective when no one sees them, so much of what they do remains guarded, for obvious reasons. They select and train soldiers at the very top of their game. Mental sharpness and adaptability under extreme stress and fatigue are the basis on which a Special Forces soldier is selected. Doing this well demonstrates huge character and personal leadership. The physical side is often what people imagine – carrying huge weight over miles of harsh mountain terrain – but any serving soldier will tell you that this is just to get to the start line. After that the real job starts. Selectors care less about whether you can get to the top of the mountain and more about how mentally sharp you are when you get there. A Special Forces soldier isn't a thug or a brute; rather he must apply intelligence and focus in the most challenging of circumstances.

The demands placed upon these individuals is made all the greater by the fact that they work in such small teams. Whereas in the regular army you might have a platoon of 30 soldiers, Special Forces teams are small and agile – maybe only four or five people. This gives them maximum impact for minimum exposure. But it also means that each individual is expected to do what several regular soldiers might do. The expectation is that the Special Forces soldier will be fitter and faster, carry more weaponry and equipment, and fire more accurately with every shot they take.

Combat is also a lot more complex than it used to be. It has changed so much over the past 20 years, in part because of the advances in technology, with so much more information to process, interpret and act upon. Special Forces might find themselves in civilian environments much more than they used to, and this brings greater challenges. Raiding military compounds in remote areas of Afghanistan is a very different prospect from operating on a busy city street, near schools, offices and shops. Gone are the days when the enemy wore their own uniform to help them stand out; now soldiers must rely on more subtle visual cues and behaviours to identify their targets. This makes acute judgement of your surroundings, sensory awareness and sharp decision making essential mental components to layer on top of technical skills.

Part of what makes this possible is the closeness of the team. Special Forces are reliant on the togetherness of their members, the clarity of their mission, the clarity of everyone's roles in achieving that mission, and the collective trust in one another's ability to do their job to the highest level of skill. Deviation or lack of discipline in any of these areas puts them all in greater danger.

In the oceans, cities and mountains in which they operate, these soldiers experience the symptoms of stress like any other person. Adrenaline, rapid heart rate, quickness of breath and blood pumping to the muscles. Despite the tangible danger of situations they find themselves in, Special Forces soldiers are not immune to their own mortality. They can't afford to be – staying alive is the first ingredient of mission success. However, the extreme nature of every challenge they face serves to channel their focus towards the skills and procedures they have practised incessantly, leaving little space to ponder their fate.

This makes day-to-day success a very Inside-Out affair for these guys – it's all about the relentless pursuit of world-class basics. It's these basics that form the building blocks of complex missions, taking every opportunity to tip the odds in their favour.

At the core of any basic skill carried out under pressure lies the ability to control your mind and body – your psychology and physiology. There exists a select group of specialist marksmen within the Special Forces who are capable of hitting a target not much bigger than a cigarette packet at 75 metres – in under one second. Indeed, every specialist role has its unique set of phenomenally high standards.

But their ability to repeat these standards under varying levels of stress and fatigue will require a soldier to channel their attention back to the very essence of control: focus on their sights, the feel of their trigger, the rhythm of their breath and the relaxation of their muscles. Any deviation or inconsistency at this base level will ripple from the Inside Out. This inconsistency from within is mirrored by the inconsistency of the shot itself, the bullet deviating more and more from its intended path with every metre it travels.

Perhaps there is no greater test of how your mind and body coalesce than coming into contact with the enemy for the first time. This is something I never thought I would actually experience when I turned up on my first day of training at the Royal Military Academy Sandhurst. I knew what the job entailed – at least I thought I did. My father served during the Second World War (he was 68 years old when I arrived into the world!) and he fought as a company commander in the D-Day landings. This put things into perspective when I joined, at a point in time when the army had very few operational commitments. And then, just two days after arriving at Sandhurst, the planes flew into the Twin Towers. A new world dawned, as did the reality and responsibility of being an officer in the British Army.

In 2004, at the age of 23, I was a young and inexperienced platoon commander on the front line in Iraq. On a routine patrol along what became known as the 'red route' in Basra (I will let you guess why), a rocket-propelled grenade exploded just ahead of our team. My physical response to that moment was unsurprising – my heart was pounding so hard it felt as though it was trying to escape my chest and a massive wave of adrenaline went coursing through my body.

But it was my mental response that surprised me more. Everything slowed down as I tuned into my surroundings with a bizarre degree of clarity. My senses were clearly alive to the situation, but in a very joined-up, coherent way. Within seconds I was able to secure our position and send a full contact report (a list of essential information) back to base. Strangely, sending a simple contact report was something I had never achieved without making mistakes in training, but in this high-stress moment my mind and body were giving me resources I didn't realise I had.

Part of the body's stress response in extreme situations involves a sharp increase in our speed of cognition, thereby giving me the impression that events on the ground were happening in slow motion. This was a phenomenally helpful and powerful tool for someone who was trying to process so much information in one moment. The whole experience reinforced something I had learned as a psychologist – that stress was not my enemy, it was my friend. But only if you embrace it as part of the experience and only if you are well prepared for that moment. People at the very top of their game generally share this positive relationship with stress, harnessing the flow of adrenaline to sharpen their trained senses and strengthen their resolve.

By setting our own challenging missions in life, pressure becomes part and parcel of our everyday experience. If it's not physical pressure then it's mental pressure – sticking to deadlines, fear of failure, fear of looking stupid, high standards, desire to improve, opportunity for recognition, opportunity for promotion or financial reward. Our body reacts to these pressures by generating energy inside us to fuel these demands, making us feel nervous or excited. This state of activation is what we commonly refer to as stress, but in this book I will also describe it as 'intensity', which frames more positively what we all feel when we are busy hustling and chasing our goals.

To master this intensity as part of your inner game, you need to have the mental, emotional and physiological range to deal with life's host of different stressors. For many people, it's not just the pressure to perform that challenges high performance. Other physiological factors such as sleep deprivation, physical exhaustion, pain, hunger, dehydration and isolation are common foes for people trying to push their limits. This range of stressors can seriously distort your thoughts, your skill, your temperament and your discipline – if you let them. And many of these stressors are more common than you might think in normal work environments. Yet we seem reluctant to accept these things as common reasons for under-performance – which they are.

If success in the Thinking Dimension is about training and managing your mind, then success in the Feeling Dimension is about managing your physiological state, such that you can deal effectively with nerves and optimise your energy. In the first half of this section we will explore why some people are able to push themselves further than others, sustaining their best performance as they go. In the second half we will focus on 'training our nerve'. This is where we learn how to achieve highly effective states of mind and body and how to maintain them under immense pressure.

13
Limits: sustaining performance on the edge

In the Introduction, I spoke about an inflection point where controlled excitement gives way to raw panic as the emotional centre of the brain (the limbic system) overrides the signals from the rational brain (the frontal lobes) responsible for our sense of control and focus. This inflection point is known by scientists as the point of catastrophe – a rather apt name. Actors and musicians call it stage fright, athletes call it choking. In a moment of intensity, they struggle to execute well-practised skills that normally should be straightforward. On the inside, they feel all the physical symptoms of fight-or-flight – a racing heart rate, a sinking stomach, muscular tension and sweaty palms. On the outside, this manifests itself in uncharacteristic mistakes. You may have experienced this yourself in a moment of pressure as your feelings overrun your focus. This moment of performance anxiety is perhaps more extreme in some professions where there is a distinct moment to stand up and perform.

This isn't the only way in which your mind and body might try to call an end to the game you are trying to play. Fatigue and tiredness also have an important contribution in overriding your conscious will to carry on. The overwhelming desire to give up is familiar in all walks of life, but nowhere is it tested so explicitly as in the selection of Special Forces soldiers.

The six-month selection process is undoubtedly a brutal test of mental, physical, emotional and intellectual stamina which only 5 per cent will see to the end. But, perhaps surprisingly, the majority of potential recruits are not failed by the directing staff; instead they voluntarily withdraw from the process. I asked a serving member who had overseen the process for many years what their top tip would be for anyone undertaking selection. He simply replied: 'Show up every day.'

His response took me back somewhat. I was expecting something far more gritty, yet there was a profound simplicity to it. It begged the question: why is turning up every day so difficult when they start the process so primed and motivated? The obvious answer would be that physical exhaustion eventually gets the better of them; their bodies simply get to a point where they can't carry on anymore. After all, surely if you could go on, you would? But, in reality, science is suggesting the physical fatigue may not be the determinant of failure, after all.

In studies where athletes are pushed to their limits in an attempt to find their 'breaking point' it has become clear that they are not, as originally thought, running out of oxygen. Neither are their muscles running out of the fundamental resources that keep them working – glycogen, fat and ATP (the source of energy within our cells).

Tim Noakes, a sports physiologist at the University of Cape Town, actually found that at the point at which cyclists claimed they felt too fatigued to continue, they were never recruiting more than about 50 per cent of their available muscle fibres.[1] Exhaustion forced them to stop exercising, yet they had a large reserve of muscle waiting to be used. So if it's not muscular fatigue pushing athletes and soldiers to their perceived limit, what is it?

Along with his colleague, Alan St Clair Gibson, Noakes proposed that the feeling of fatigue is imposed centrally, by the brain.[2] In other words, the brain invents the sensory and emotional conditions of fatigue before the muscles reach actual breaking point – a mechanism which makes perfect sense in survival terms. Shutting down physical activity in advance of a complete system failure ensures a safe margin of error and means you can continue to function even after an exhausting challenge.[3]

It makes sense to me as a psychologist that by changing your mental response you can change your physical response. This is, after all, why belief and choice are so fundamental to performing at your best. This idea that fatigue and the desire to give up are governed by the brain's 'central governor' rather than the heart, lungs or muscles is illustrated by the known impact of performance-enhancing drugs such as amphetamines, modafinil and caffeine, all of which influence the central nervous system and not the muscles.

I can imagine a few moral dilemmas in the future if we are able to override this 'safety mechanism' of the brain – mentally or with drugs – in order to push ourselves to actual biological exhaustion. Where human determination meets extreme conditions there is a fine line between life and death, whether that's lack of oxygen on Mount Everest, cold exposure in the Arctic or dehydration in ultra-distance athletes.

Sadly, those most in danger of exceeding human limits are not the small number of people climbing Everest or crossing deserts, they are the huge number of people pushing themselves to burnout in every-day jobs. The people who are slowly taking more out of the tank than they are putting in. Your mind and body are capable of giving you so much, but if you expose them to relentless demands and never stop to fill the tank, they can only go so far. This is the real danger.

Striking the balance between stress and recovery

Once you start drawing from an empty tank, you may as well forget high performance; your body is in survival mode. For example, a 2 per cent loss in hydration has been equated to a 20 per cent loss in concentration – yet how easy is it to get to the end of the day having forgotten to drink enough water, especially in the winter when you don't feel the need to hydrate as much? The people cycling across continents and rowing across oceans are fine because they have been planning their self-management for months – they know exactly what they are going to eat and drink and exactly when they are going to consume it. They even have alarm clocks reminding them when to eat and drink, as well as an abundance of techniques to help them deal with the psychological challenges they are likely to encounter.

The people we should be far more concerned about are the ones confined to a desk for 14 hours a day, enduring relentless low-level stress, rising cortisol levels (the primary stress hormone) and periodic spikes of adrenaline which, without exercise, translates into tension and high blood pressure. It's these people who are more likely to forget to eat proper meals and drink enough water – often in the name of ambition.

Simon Jeffries left the Royal Marines in 2015, having also served with UK Special Forces for much of his career. He was an excellent soldier, winning the esteemed King's Badge for outstanding performance within the service. Reflecting on his transition from the world of Special Forces to the corporate world when I interviewed him for this book, he described the stress as very different – but not in the way you might imagine. He recognised that, for many people, combat operations in Afghanistan may sound very stressful, but in fact he described it as a 'simplified world with no distractions'. The environment was complex, but the mission was singular. He and his team were in and out of short periods of high intensity matched equally with periods of recovery and rest. Recovery periods weren't long – generally they had missions most nights – but mini-recoveries can be very effective for maintaining optimal performance. Managed well, this 'pressure–release' cycle is actually what strengthens the capacity for stress over time (something we cover in Section 4, Training your nerve).

To enable this process, Simon had a disciplined routine that ensured he maximised both intensity and recovery. He was eating properly and remained physically fit. He recalls being part of a close-knit team who looked out for one another and lifted each other's spirits when required. He reckoned he probably laughed about 30 times a day.

In contrast, when he left the military to work in the city, his experience was very different. The balance of stress and recovery was tilted heavily in favour of being permanently connected, so much so that he struggled to ever optimise his performance or find a sustainable routine. The culture didn't allow it. Instead, working late was expected, especially if everyone else was doing it. There was little mission clarity, which meant it was less about working towards a well-defined outcome and more about being seen to do the right things. If you're not exhausted, you must be doing something wrong.

For first-year Goldman Sachs analysts, an 80-hour work week would be considered a dream. Instead, apparently, their average work week is 95 hours or more, according to an internal survey that went viral.[4] The survey of 13 first-year analysts showed that they slept an average of five hours a night. They rated their physical and mental health at below 3 on a scale of 1 to 10; their personal life got a rock-bottom 1 on the scale. On the bright side, only 17 per cent said they frequently experienced shouting or swearing.

It's tempting to dismiss or mock complaints from new recruits fresh out of university making six figures, with the prospect of even higher future income. But when the COVID-19 pandemic disrupted the way millions of white-collar professionals around the world go about their jobs, companies were exposed for the way they manage their human capital.

In 2019 Microsoft conducted an experiment in Japan, a culture known for its extremely long working hours. It gave its employees five consecutive three-day weekends. Astonishingly, Microsoft's sales per employee soared by 40 per cent from the previous year.[5] The company also saved money on energy bills and paper-copying costs. There are plenty of reasons to believe that this was no fluke. An experiment at the New Zealand firm Perpetual Guardian produced similar results when employees worked only four days a week for two months.[6] In addition, research by Stanford University economist John Pencavel on British munitions plant workers during the First World War found that, past a certain point, working more decreases hourly output.[7]

It's not hard to think of some reasons for this to happen: physical and mental fatigue affecting the end of one day and carrying over into the next day; many people's jobs are never finished – there is always something useful to be done. Therefore it's easy to get into the habit of filling in the time in an unproductive manner, waiting for the end of the day. A third reason might be social signalling. This is when employees make themselves look busy in order to appease their co-workers. Who would want to work efficiently if it meant being labelled as lazy at the end of the day when you had nothing important to do? Better to just keep telling everyone how busy you are and go home late just to prove it.

It would seem therefore that Microsoft's experiment of simply shortening the work week might have legs. France, for example, has a 35-hour work week and 35 days of paid annual leave. Unsurprisingly, France has one of the higher levels of productivity per hour in the developed world.

Self-care before mental toughness

Long hours are a badge of honour for many city workers. Tech firms are now taking over from the banks in terms of propagating a 'survival of the fittest' mentality to performance. Don't get me wrong, there is no doubt that dedication and mental toughness are valuable qualities in any organisation looking for its employees to consistently over-perform – but to what end?

For our Special Forces soldier, many missions are protracted over a period of weeks, even months, so it would be easy to allow a fair amount of stress to prevail as a constant. Mental toughness, or grit, is certainly important in maintaining this effectiveness – it's essential to know that you are capable of staying effective and doing the basics well when you are physically and mentally exhausted. But if you rely on mental toughness at the expense of micro-recovery – which comes from an attitude of self-care and sustainability – then you will be limiting your potential considerably.

A great example of this came from one of the Special Forces' most senior and experienced directing staff. What he didn't know about training for combat wasn't worth knowing. He shared with me a story that clearly resonated with him a great deal, yet it wasn't a war story about their heroics in a far-flung part of the world. Instead, it was a story about the quality of beds in the army training camp at Sennybridge in Wales.

He had finally won a long-running argument to get the mattresses changed as the present ones had been affecting the quality of the troops' sleep when they were on exercise. He had been pushed back a number of times, told that if anyone should be capable of operating off of a poor night's sleep it should be the SAS. This had clearly irritated him, as you could see from how he was telling the story. His point was simple but profound – the soldiers' job is demanding enough without having to layer in unnecessary challenges. By reducing their opportunity to sleep well they were diminishing their capacity to learn important technical skills, skills that required their undivided attention.

This is what athletes call 'training effect', which is about isolating the specific component of performance you are trying to get better at in order to maximise the impact of your effort. Therefore a poor night's sleep in the name of mental toughness was, in this case, self-defeating in achieving the correct training effect. This may have been a different story if the training effect was to test the soldiers' skills while sleep deprived – which may be the next level of challenge – in which case they probably wouldn't be sleeping indoors!

As the barrier between work and rest becomes blurred, maybe even non-existent for some people, you run the risk of doing irreparable damage. This isn't just about performance, it ends up being about survival. This is especially true of people who work shift patterns or irregular hours where they struggle to anchor their body's all-important ebbs and flows to a regular routine.

It's important to remember that, just because your job isn't physically demanding, it doesn't mean it's not physiologically demanding. An athlete or soldier will experience a far greater physical load on their body than, say, a financial trader or an air-traffic controller who might be sitting down for most of their day. However, the financial trader and air-traffic controller may well experience higher levels of physiological stress in the form of nervous energy, despite being less mobile. Indeed, sometimes being less mobile is paradoxically the reason for experiencing more stress.

In fact, the demands on executives to sustain high performance, day in, day out and year on year, dwarf the challenges faced by any athlete or soldier I have worked with in this regard. A professional athlete, and indeed a Special Forces soldier, will spend 95 per cent of their time training and 5 per cent of their time competing or on operations. This gives them plenty of opportunity to find their optimum performance. Athletes even enjoy an off-season while Special Forces soldiers have a rotation system that offers them relative predictability in their balance of training and operations.

Executives, however, are lucky if it's the reverse, spending 95 per cent of their time competing and 5 per cent of their time training and recovering. And this might continue relentlessly for a full career of 40 years. While it's not always within your power to change your external environment, you can always get better at changing your inner state.

Simon's experience brilliantly highlights the difference between short-term (acute) and long-term (chronic) stress, where acute stress raises your game for the moment you are in and chronic stress allows you to get up every day and keep going. As Simon's story highlighted, the way we're designed means that we perform brilliantly under short-term physical stress but very poorly under long-term psychological stress.

Either way, it's the opportunity to 'release' from intensity (even for short moments in a day) that determines your longevity. Stress guzzles energy, no matter how positive the experience; therefore without effective recovery you can only go on for so long. And you can't take fuel from an empty tank.

Sleep – the panacea of recovery

The story above neatly highlights the single biggest player in performance recovery: sleep. This is so intrinsic to our performance that it's almost pointless working on other areas of performance psychology until you are able to achieve high-quality sleep. When Usain Bolt was asked what was the most important part of his training routine, he simply replied, 'Sleep.' He's not the only one. Tennis player Roger Federer famously sleeps 11–12 hours per night, and Jeff Bezos, founder of Amazon and now the world's wealthiest person, has also spoken of his zero-compromise stance on sleep. In particular, Bezos recognises the impact it has on the quality of his decision making, something he attributes to Amazon's phenomenal success.

Research into the effects of sleep has increased exponentially over the past 20 years because of the profound importance it has on our mental and physical performance as well as our health. The effect of sleep deprivation is thought to cost businesses in the United States more than $100 billion a year. The ability to 'survive' on five hours of sleep a night has been celebrated among high-profile figures, including politicians. Until we reverse this culture and demonstrate the importance of good sleep hygiene, we are not only severely limiting our human potential but also fanning the flames of a mental health crisis.

Sleep works on a number of levels in the brain. Toxins, including those associated with Alzheimer's disease, are flushed out during sleep. Sleep solidifies our memory. It enhances high-level mental processing as well as creativity. It fends off depression and low mood. The restorative effects of sleep are important for anyone, but in high-performing environments you are drawing on huge reserves of mental and physical energy that have to be replenished if you are to stand any chance of sustaining that high performance.

Essential to training good sleep hygiene seems to be the 'golden hour' before bed. This is when good sleepers are able to wind down in a consistent way, maybe reading or taking a bath. Digital devices are the biggest no-no. The blue light suppresses the production of melatonin in your brain which is essential for going to sleep. Emails and social media also generate low-level stress that activates your nervous system and delays the onset of sleep. In contrast, meditation and simple breathing exercises help our nervous system to slow down and can facilitate a much deeper sleep.

Importantly, you needn't obsess about how much sleep you got in any one night. Think more in terms of a moving average over the past five days where a few nights of less sleep is fine, so long as you are able to make up for it at some point. I always tell athletes not to worry if they don't get any sleep before a big competition – so long as they are generally well rested, they will still be able to perform. Ironically, this advice often helps them to relax and sleep well!

Sleeping needn't focus on night-time either. Short naps during the day are now recognised as being tremendously beneficial. When Manchester United won the treble in 1998–99 they had been the first team to introduce dedicated napping facilities into their training ground, as well as employing a specialist sleep coach.

If sleep is our primary source of recovery, it's also important you identify opportunities for micro-recovery. These are small behavioural changes that allow you to conserve your energy more efficiently during the day. This is something I take very seriously when working with individuals who are away from home working, training or serving for long periods. When working with the Winter Olympic team it became clear that over the course of a long season, most of it away from home, athletes and staff started to lose energy and focus.

The intense routine of training and competing was difficult to sustain, and the high-performance habits – which everyone was fully committed to at the beginning of the season – started to fall apart by the end of the season. It wasn't long before this started to affect results.

The next season I challenged the team to collectively identify 100 small things that would help us to maintain positive mood, energy, focus and relationships. Interestingly, near the top of the list was the importance of changing out of team kit to have dinner every evening. Team kit felt like uniform for many of the athletes, and as long as they were in uniform, they were on duty. Changing into their own clothes gave them a mental break from the pressure of being an athlete so they could switch off and just be themselves. Another small example was having hand sanitisers at every entrance and exit to reduce risk of illness and colds, something which can set back an athlete's fitness by weeks (a habit that people now take far more seriously since the COVID-19 pandemic).

14
Performance anxiety: living with fear and expectation

Avicii was one of the most talented and prolific DJs and producers the world has ever seen, with his unique dance music and melodies loved by millions. For many reasons I wish I had known Tim Bergling – his real name – before his death in 2018 at the age of 28. Distress and panic were eating him up from the inside out.[1]

Avicii, or Tim as he was still known back then, had been noticed as a teenager for his immense talent for writing music, attracting the attention of agents and managers. The Swede was quickly picked up and propelled towards superstardom. He put 100 per cent into his craft, which was split into two activities – writing music and performing music. But it was the creative process of writing that Avicii really loved. He could happily spend days, weeks, even months collaborating with artists and producing spell-binding melodies, always with impeccable attention to detail. Nile Rodgers once said of working with Avicii that he was 'one of the greatest natural melody writers the world has ever seen'. Avicii's 'Wake Me Up' spent 26 weeks at the top of the US billboard chart for dance singles and the DJ also made music with the likes of Madonna and Coldplay.

I've spent hours on YouTube watching videos of Avicii making his music. As you observe him sitting there at his computer and layering different components of the track, you can start to see how his mind works. He would listen to something and immediately connect it with a melody or a tune that he might have heard six months ago and which was stored in one of thousands of files on his computer. He would go straight to that file. Only through intrinsic passion and love do we create that mental architecture that allows us to perform so intuitively, to create and join connections in our head. This is a perfect illustration of how the Thinking Dimension (his mental process) meets the Intuitive Dimension (his unconscious autopilot). If you watch those YouTube videos, you can see Avicii is in a deep state of flow, similar to the state I described at the beginning of this book.

When writing music, Avicii was the archetypal example of what it means to be intrinsically motivated – doing it for the pure love of it and rewarded as much by the process as the outcome. An introverted and intuitive character, his personality type lent itself well to working in small groups and enjoying the intimate nature of collaborating with other talented artists. It was here where he had the most fun and the most energy.

Performing live concerts was a different matter. At first he felt the buzz of having tens of thousands of adoring fans sing along to his music. It was an opportunity to enjoy the expression of his work. This wasn't his natural habitat, however. Each concert was quite literally 'a performance'. He could rise to it because it was novel, it was exciting and he had the energy to be the extrovert his fans wanted him to be on stage. But as shows came thick and fast, his energy started to wane. Positive energy turned into negative anxiety as his body become reliant on cortisol-driven stress to get to the end of the night. As a young man experiencing global fame, his only support network was his management team who would tell him to 'make the most of the opportunity he had'. Tim performed an average of three concerts per week over three years, travelling constantly. This was on top of daily media appearances and interviews, in themselves energy sapping for an introverted personality. Despite all of this, he still had to write new music, with the pressure of making every track as big as the one before it. Having never really touched alcohol, Tim started to have a few drinks before each concert to try to numb the anxiety.

Tim was in Australia in the middle of a world tour when he was rushed to hospital with severe pain in the stomach. He was diagnosed with pancreatitis, a response to intense, prolonged stress. He ended up having his appendix and gall bladder removed.

As a performance psychologist, I find the documentary about his life, *Avicii: True Stories*, incredibly insightful. There are some fascinating and touching moments where he offers a lot about what he's thinking and what's going on inside his head. It's a brilliant illustration of how thoughts and feelings can interact to devastating effect.

Still Avicii carried on performing, medicated up to the eyeballs. He described how he was living a happiness that wasn't his own and that what he really should have done was stop so he could take some time out to get over the stress. When he did eventually take some months off from touring, he found himself incapable of working out in the gym. Every time his heart rate increased, his threat response kicked in and he suffered anxiety attacks. The association between a high heart rate and the panic he felt whenever he was about to go on stage had been reinforced over and over again. His brain's limbic system become conditioned to interpret anything that raised his heart rate – including exercise – as an assault, and the same threat response ensued. These are exactly the same symptoms seen in soldiers returning from Iraq and Afghanistan with post-traumatic stress.

Having taken time out to rediscover his love for writing and producing music, Avicii thought he would be okay to perform again. But things got worse. In the moments before he went on stage he wasn't breathing; instead, he was holding his breath and physically shaking. The second he stepped up in front of the audience he was hit again by anxiety and panic – an acute stress response that had now been deeply conditioned. After a long fight with his management team, he eventually stopped performing live concerts in an attempt to take back his life.

Tragically, Tim's life came to an end on 20 April 2018, with his death reported as suicide. His was the story of a young man who had suffered intolerably for his talent and success.

I believe there are important lessons that we can take from Avicii's tragic tale. This story hit me hard, knowing how much we can do to change our relationship with stress. Too many people feel forced to step aside from the profession or sport they love because of performance anxiety. And it doesn't need to be that way.

There's always so much we can do to mitigate the negative effects of stress – as we continue to explore in the Feeling Dimension. The problem is that, in order to transform the way your mind and body respond to the demands placed upon you, you need to condition new strategies into the very fabric of your daily routines. If you are doing them only in response to feeling stressed, you are missing the point. This is especially true for peak stress events like performing live on stage, where artists need to incorporate deliberate performance strategies and routines in the same way that top athletes do.

For Avicii, the problem sadly grew too big over time, but in the early stages what he felt would have been normal for anyone performing on stage to that many people. It's an example of how eustress (euphoric stress) can soon turn into distress if you start to make negative associations with high-pressure situations. As a result you become more and more anxious when you think about the next performance, forgetting to breathe, stay relaxed and focus on your blueprint.

In Section 4, 'Training your nerve', I will share my systematic way of conditioning calm, focused states (coherence) with high-pressure events. But before that I want to explore the relationship between stress and performance in more detail, as this will give you some valuable insights into what exactly it is that you are trying to get better at.

15
Challenge: finding an alternative to fight-or-flight

I started to really appreciate the complex relationship between stress and performance when I went back to the University of Bath to work with the athletes from my own sport of modern pentathlon.

I had retired from the Great Britain team a few years earlier, and during that time there had been a significant change to the format of the sport. As the oldest Olympic sport, modern pentathlon has had its fair share of, well, modernising. The latest change was designed to make the sport more exciting and spectator friendly, which it certainly did. Two of the events, the shooting and the running, were combined to create a winter biathlon-style event. This now involves running four 800-metre loops, and between each loop athletes run onto a shooting range. They shoot at a target 10 metres away, which they must hit five times before they are allowed to embark on their next 800-metre loop.

As you might imagine, this was a considerable change for the athletes who had only ever trained the two disciplines separately. There is an ocean of difference between shooting in a quiet hall taking 20 shots over a 30-minute period compared with running onto the range with a large crowd booing and cheering your every move while you are trying to maintain the composure to shoot accurately, with your muscles shaking and your heart pounding at 150 beats per minute.

There couldn't have been a better activity to conduct my research on mind–body performance, and helping me out were a stellar cast of athletes including Kate French and Joseph Choong, who both went on to win gold medals at the Tokyo Olympics, Olympic silver medallist Sam Murray and World Champion Jamie Cooke. The research was simple. I wanted to see what factors affected their performance the most – cognitive anxiety (the amount they worried about their performance) or somatic stress (the physiological demand they were under, as measured by their heart rate). Each athlete was required to run on a treadmill until they reached the desired heart rate, at which point they would jump off and conduct the shooting exercise. This involved hitting the target five times as quickly as they could, just as they would have to in competition.

The results were fascinating. Initially, it was clear that cognitive anxiety had a significant impact on the athletes' shooting performance, regardless of how much stress their body was under. The more worry they reported, the less well they performed. This didn't come as any surprise given what we know about how anxiety can inhibit attentional control in the prefrontal lobes of the brain. If they were worried about their performance, then it follows that they would have fewer attentional resources to focus fully on the shooting task.

What was more insightful (and less expected) were the results for somatic stress. Remember, this was measured by their heart rate and therefore how much stress their body was under. Contrary to what I was expecting, their heart rate seemed to have very little impact on their performance. I couldn't believe this. Intuitively, it made little sense when we know how intense exercise can limit our attentional resources in the brain, especially when the exercise being measured requires fine motor movement. The lowest heart rate they were tested at was 80 beats per minute and the highest was 140 beats per minute, so initially I wondered if this was enough of a range to make a difference in athletes who were well trained in this particular skill.

But then, out of curiosity, I decided to test another variable. As well as measuring their somatic stress, I also measured their somatic stress *direction*. This is a measure of how much they *believe* that physical fatigue will impact their performance negatively. If they believed that physical fatigue made little difference to their ability to shoot, then they scored low on this scale. If they believed that physical fatigue made a big difference to their shooting ability, then they scored high. The simple change was illuminating. Those who believed that somatic stress affects performance negatively scored significantly worse compared to those who believed that somatic stress makes little difference, and when combined with high cognitive anxiety they were by far the worst group.

This suggests that it's not the actual presence of stress that stops us from performing at our best; rather it's whether we *believe* that these sensations are bad for us.

This idea was backed up by a landmark study conducted at Stanford University[1] where the researchers measured the impact of stress in 30,000 participants over eight years. The conclusions defied the previous assumptions of many about stress – in particular that stress is bad for us. Participants were split into two groups: those who experienced routine high stress and those who experienced routine low stress. After eight years the researchers measured mortality rates in both groups and found no difference between the groups in those more likely to suffer stress-related illness. However, they also asked the participants about whether they believed stress was good or bad for them. It turned out that those who believed that stress was bad for them were 43 per cent more likely to die of stress-related disease than those who didn't believe it was bad for them – regardless of how much stress they were actually under. In fact, the researchers found that people experiencing high stress but with a positive attitude to stress were less likely to die than those under low stress with a negative attitude. In addition, people's perception of stress was more predictive of whether or not they would die than any other socio-economic factor.

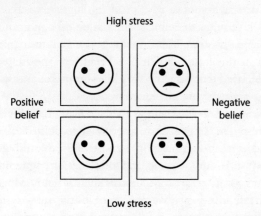

FIGURE 15.1 The relationship between stress and our belief about stress

This study clearly suggests that the amount of stress you are under bears less relation to whether you will suffer any stress-related illness than you might think. However, if you believe that stress is bad for you, you are significantly more likely to suffer illness, or even die from stress-related causes.

This study also reinforced what I had discovered in sport – that stress and pressure are not the enemies in how you perform; rather, it's your belief that mediates the impact of stress. This makes your knowledge and confidence around stress essential to how it affects you.

Practising your challenge response

It turns out that by reappraising your attitude to stress and the sensations of stress you can influence real physiological shifts in your body. This could be as simple as repeating to yourself, 'I feel excited', rather than 'I feel scared'. These two statements create very different bio-resilience profiles inside us. Both are associated with an increase in heart rate and butterflies in the stomach, but when you are excited about an event (eustress), the major arteries stay dilated, meaning that the blood pressure stays low. When you are scared (distress), the major arteries constrict, resulting in increased blood pressure. Over time this can cause heart disease and other health complications. Furthermore, a positive mental response to a challenging event – the 'challenge response' – is thought to facilitate the biological conditions in which the heart actually strengthens, making you better adapted to deal with stress in the future. So maybe Friedrich Nietzsche was right when he declared that 'what doesn't kill you makes you stronger'. So long as you practise your challenge response.

This research is so compelling that scientists now belief that this challenge response is the positive alternative to fight-or-flight. Where fight-or-flight is a coping response and therefore limiting, our challenge response is empowering and therefore strengthening. What's more, thanks to the efforts of scientists such as Andy Morgan, a psychiatrist at Yale University, we may have found the very mechanism within the body that helps to differentiate these positive and negative responses.[2]

Of all the training that Special Forces soldiers undergo, resistance to interrogation is commonly accepted to be the toughest. Sleep deprived and forced to endure stress positions and brutal questioning from their mock captors, scientists have witnessed in these soldiers the highest levels of cortisol ever measured in humans. So what's the difference between those who can tolerate these extreme conditions and stay effective versus those who cannot?

The answer would seem to be in a relatively untested hormone called DHEA (dehydroepiandrosterone) produced in the body's adrenal glands. Soldiers most effective during high-stress interrogation all showed peaks of DHEA in conjunction with cortisol. This seems to help them filter potentially harmful experiences, thereby reducing the negative impact and helping them to stay effective and in control during the experience. It also reduces their likelihood of trauma afterwards.

Interestingly, post-traumatic stress is associated not only with lower levels of DHEA but also with lower cortisol and adrenaline levels. This sounds surprising given that you may expect trauma to be associated with more stress hormone, not less, but this suggests that these soldiers somehow haven't 'completed' the appropriate stress response. Just like the 'suppresser' group in the study I mentioned earlier when people had to watch a gruesome video of surgery, they are likely to be inhibiting the feeling of stress rather than letting it play out and staying positively focused through the process.

If so, this reinforces the importance of proactively training your challenge response as an alternative to fight-or-flight. As well as reframing fear as excitement, you must not ignore your emotions or push them down; rather, you should acknowledge them and let them play out. At the same time you must learn to control your focus and your breathing while staying positive and proactive. All of this we will cover in much more detail a little further on, and I will give you some ways in which you can test and strengthen this challenge response in a safe and controlled way.

16

Emotions: know your feelings, know your performance

One other important technique that seems to propagate our challenge response is how we use self-talk to guide our thoughts and emotions. Morgan's research has found that this impacts our neurobiological response.

One of the roles of a psychologist in the field of high performance is simply to encourage people to talk about their experiences, their ideas, their decisions, their processes, their emotions and so on. Essentially, by being encouraged to talk out loud they are forced to order and prioritise their thoughts and proactively deal with the challenges and emotions that stand in their way. By doing this they develop greater confidence in being able to deal with these challenges and emotions; therefore it follows that they will have greater confidence in their challenge response. But to do this you must truly own your performance.

Imagine a player walks off the pitch having had a bad game. Maybe they have made a few silly mistakes that cost their team the win. They may well be experiencing some strong feelings, although exactly which feelings tells us a lot about how they are appraising the situation. For example, if they report feeling angry, it suggests they are attributing their poor performance to something or someone else – maybe the referee made a bad decision or a teammate wasn't giving them good service. If, however, they report feeling guilty, it suggests they are internalising their poor performance and blaming themselves. Similarly, they might be feeling frustrated, confused, unlucky or unworthy. All of these feelings play a subtly different tune inside us and lead to different outcomes, different lessons, different conversations, different goals for next time.

Without knowing this information all you see is their behaviour, which could be punching a wall, launching their shoes across the changing room, screaming and shouting, or maybe just quietly with-drawing, sitting on their own in the corner of the room and not saying anything. In other words, their behaviour is a crude proxy for what's going on in their mind and body. To be able to understand their behaviour and do something useful with it you need to under-stand how they feel. This is just as important for positive emotions as well. Someone who feels grateful or lucky is clearly appraising the situation very differently from someone who feels proud or satisfied, even though the observable behaviours might look the same.

The real challenge comes when people can't express their emotions effectively, maybe because they can't find the right words or because they are just not tuned into them in the first place. Instead, they use generic statements like 'It was good' or 'I am pleased because we won'. Again, in order to reinforce positive performance in the future you have to be able to extract something a little more tangible. To help do this you might need to start with logic before you explore feeling. A realistic progression of coaching questions to ask yourself might be:

- What happened?
- What did I expect to happen?
- What changed?
- What impact did that have on me?
- How did that impact my ability to think clearly/stay relaxed/stay positive/stay energised?
- How would the best version of me have dealt with that?

These questions all help to draw out not just what happened objec-tively but your experience of what happened – how events affected you and your ability to perform at your best. The more accurately you can name these emotions, the more you can pinpoint their effects – positive or negative. But, by sitting on your emotions, you incubate them, so you shouldn't be surprised when they keep grow-ing – along with the impact they have on your behaviour. Naming your emotions tends to be the best way of diffusing their charge and reducing the burden they create. To paraphrase psychologist Dan Siegel, 'Name it to tame it.'

Most work environments don't give much regard to this component of human performance. At best they may adopt an after-action review process to better understand what made a project successful or not, but the human experience of the project rarely gets discussed, even though it undoubtedly would have played a huge role. Many work environments prefer that you park emotions at the door on the way in so they don't get in the way. This is a sure-fire way of stifling performance over time as you start to put more unconscious energy into suppressing the emotional outlay of challenging relationships and self-doubt. This may protect you from the discomfort of a difficult situation, but it also prevents you from experiencing positive performance emotions that are essential to being at your very best – emotions such as excitement, commitment, pride and purpose.

Over time you tune out of what's going on in your body. This is a problem because a large part of your emotional regulation comes down to being able to differentiate between sensations within your body. You then have to take this information and link it to your interpretation of what's going on around you. Therefore, if you are no good at recognising your emotions, you will be no good at accurately interpreting what's going on around you.

This was brilliantly demonstrated in one of my favourite psychology experiments. The Capilano Suspension Bridge in North Vancouver was the scene for this enlightening study, which was designed to test our ability to interpret our emotions.[1] Two hundred and thirty feet above the Capilano River and 450 feet long, the bridge consists of wooden struts attached to a swinging wire cable. As you walk across it, the bridge wobbles and sways. Standing in the middle of the bridge was a pretty female research assistant who invited male passers-by to take part in a study exploring the link between creativity and picturesque scenery. In doing so they had to write a brief story. The assistant then gave participants her contact details in case they had any follow-up questions. As well as conducting this process on the swinging bridge, she did exactly the same on a solid bridge upriver which was completely stable.

Researchers found a clear distinction in the stories of men from each bridge. Most obvious was the fact that on the swinging bridge their stories were packed with sexual content whereas on the solid bridge there was no such content. In addition, the men on the swinging bridge were much more likely to have made contact with the assistant after the study.

Since 1975, when this study was conducted, psychologists and neuroscientists have learned a lot about emotions, including how we interpret them and how we act upon them. The swinging bridge experiment therefore reinforces what we now know, that different emotions share similar bodily symptoms. Although standing on a swaying bridge does nothing to promote sexual arousal, it does promote a slight sense of fear and trepidation, which happens to share similar bodily symptoms with those our mind associates with sexual attraction – increased adrenaline, racing pulse and fast breathing. Our interpretation of these symptoms then boils down to context. When faced with a pretty research assistant, the emotions are interpreted as a rather intense attraction. So there you go – if you learn nothing else from this book, make sure you meet your next date on a wobbly bridge.

This principle reinforces an essential message when it comes to managing nerves – that as far as our physiology is concerned there is little difference between fear and excitement. The difference is how you choose to interpret it. Nerves are merely sensations we associate with our body's anticipation of an important event. Unless you convince yourself not to care about the event (not a tactic I would recommend as you will get into all sorts of mental battles), your only choice is to accept these emotions and choose how you want to interpret and frame them. This can have profound consequences, lowering blood pressure, creating more regular breathing patterns and heart rhythms, and ultimately allowing you to access your powerful challenge response.

In summary, to be resilient in the face of the common adversity and relentless intensity that come with many high-performance environments, you have to be better at understanding your emotions. That doesn't necessarily mean digging deep into early childhood experiences, as may sometimes be necessary in psychotherapy; rather, it is about recognising and then renaming the adrenaline surges that underlie all intense emotions, in a way that makes them more acceptable and manageable.

So now I want to share in more detail my systematic approach to developing emotional and physiological resilience over time, thereby conditioning ourselves to respond more effectively when the pressure is on.

Section 4: Training your nerve

Whether walking into the most important exam of your life, going up on stage in front of a large crowd or stepping up to take a penalty in the World Cup final, you will be aware of your heart pounding and your stomach churning. Very often, this abundance of energy coursing around the body may not be warranted. You hardly need excessive amounts of physical energy to sit down for a three-hour exam, but you do need a slow release of mental energy to sustain you and to maintain your concentration. This slow release of energy is not something that comes naturally to the nervous system, which prefers the extreme rapid-response approach offered by fight-or-flight. But neither fighting nor running away is particularly appropriate behaviour in an exam room. You therefore have to learn how to actively manage your physiological response, ensuring that you stay calm and relaxed, allowing your nervous energy to filter through at a more appropriate pace. By tapping into this natural energy source in the right way, you should be mentally sharper than it's possible to be compared to if there was nothing to win or lose.

This suggests that you must be okay with feeling nervous. By using the techniques I will be giving you to manage your physiology, you are *not* trying to eradicate the uncomfortable feeling of nerves – instead, you are going to accept a degree of discomfort, make friends with this feeling and turn it into something more positive.

A racing heart and churning stomach are the most common symptoms of nerves, and if you are not familiar with this feeling it can be extremely off-putting. Therefore just acknowledging this as normal can have a positive effect in itself. I work with many young children who often believe they are the only ones who experience such sensations. I love the palpable sense of relief you can see in their faces when other kids share the same experiences and they realise that they are not the only ones who get nervous.

For those people who experience pressure more regularly, nerves tend to go with the territory. Top performers don't generally get less nervous than anyone else, they just become more experienced at sitting with the sensations and channelling them into positive focus and action. They also stay physically relaxed while feeling nervous – this is a fundamental skill you have to work on, because it doesn't come naturally. What you have also learned from the previous section is that your interpretation of this feeling is more influential on your performance than the feeling itself. Nerves are neither good nor bad; they are simply energy. The goal is to stay in control – thinking effectively, acting decisively and staying relaxed despite your nerves.

My approach to 'training your nerve' has two phases:

> *Phase 1: Training coherent states.* Here you are learning how to control your physiology, achieving coherent states that help you to perform at your best.

> *Phase 2: Expanding your comfort zone (autonomic fitness).* Here I will show you how to condition these coherent states to high-stress environments so that you can maintain total focus and calm on the big occasions. This is called 'autonomic fitness'.

17
Phase 1: Training coherent states

'Coherence' is a positive state of relaxed alertness. I work on three foundation skills for achieving coherent states. It's important you can do the Three Foundations extremely well before you move on to Phase 2 where we will be introducing performance stress into the equation. The Three Foundations are:

1 Deep breathing
2 Active relaxation
3 Positive focus.

In all of my time working in the field of performance psychology, I haven't come across anything as influential to personal performance and leadership as these three foundational human skills. It's essential to establish these foundations brilliantly, and in sequence, before you introduce any stress into the system. The Three Foundations form the basis of your psycho-physiological control. Without these in place you will have no basis of consistency for anything you are trying to do. In the face of mounting pressure, this inconsistency will magnify.

Before we get into these skills, it might be helpful to share a little bit about the science of coherent states so that you know what's going on inside.

Having the heart to win

Surprisingly, the heart has a disproportionate impact on our ability to access optimal performance states. In the relatively new field of neurocardiology, scientists have discovered that the heart possesses its own intrinsic nervous system containing more than 40,000 neurons.[1]

This 'little brain' gives the heart the ability to independently sense, process information, make decisions and even demonstrate a type of learning and memory.

This debunks what most of us were taught at school – that the heart responds to 'orders' sent by the brain in the form of neural signals. As it turns out, the heart actually sends more signals to the brain than the brain sends to the heart. Moreover, these heart signals have a significant effect on brain function, influencing emotional processing as well as higher cognitive faculties such as attention, perception, memory and problem-solving. So not only does the heart respond to the brain but the brain continuously responds to the heart.

Scientists have discovered an intrinsic link between the heart's rhythms (how it speeds up and slows down over time) and being able to achieve optimal states of performance. Contrary to what you may imagine, the speed of the heart oscillates considerably over the course of a minute, gently speeding up and slowing down numerous times. If your heart-rate monitor says your heart is beating at 70 beats per minute (bpm), it's more likely to be fluctuating between 60 and 80 bpm, with 70 bpm being the average. The speed and consistency of these fluctuations give us a measure of heart rate variance (HRV). The importance of HRV has been transformational in our understanding of mind–body performance (psycho-physiology) in the world's top performers.

Driving these natural oscillations are two parts of the nervous system, the sympathetic nervous system (which accelerates the heart rate and gives us a nervous 'boost') and the parasympathetic nervous system (which slows down the heart rate and helps us to relax). Think of these as the accelerator and brake pedals. Being ready to perform means being relaxed but alert – this is when you are at your best. When you are in the optimal state of relaxed alertness, both parts of the nervous system work together in harmony, speeding up and slowing down about five times every minute. By practising the Three Foundations you are effectively 'tuning in' the nervous system, making it ready to perform.

Incoherent states

When you experience negative emotions such as fear or frustration, or you feel overwhelmed, your heart rhythms become erratic and disordered. We call this an 'incoherent' state. You can see this in Figure 17.1, which shows the HRV of an athlete before practising the Three Foundations. In this case they were imagining a high-pressure competition. This incoherent state inhibits activity in the prefrontal lobes (cortical inhibition), reducing their ability to think clearly and control the situation.

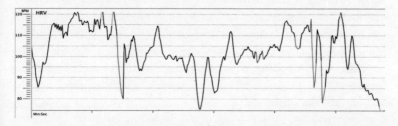

FIGURE 17.1 The heart rate variance (over 2–3 minutes) of an athlete in an incoherent state

This incoherent state has negative effects on your performance for a couple of reasons. First, if the brake and accelerator are not working in harmony, they end up fighting each other. In a car, when you apply the brake and accelerator at the same time, the car performs poorly and burns out the engine. The same is true of the nervous system – this disharmony between the sympathetic and parasympathetic nerves causes the body to operate inefficiently, deplete your energy and throwing many of the body's systems off-kilter.

Second, this complex feedback loop between heart and brain works both ways, meaning that irregularity in your heart rhythm is associated with suboptimal functioning of the brain's frontal lobes, reducing cognitive performance. Similarly, if you lack focus because you are underprepared, or you haven't set clear goals, or the demands of what you are doing are simply too much, this will weaken the strength of signal from the frontal lobes – opening the door for your stress response. The more extreme and more prolonged this incoherent state, the greater impact it will have on your performance.

Coherent states

In contrast, positive emotions such as excitement and pride, combined with techniques such as deep breathing and visualisation, send a very different signal throughout your body. This creates heart rhythm patterns that are highly ordered as the sympathetic and parasympathetic nervous systems work in harmony, allowing you to be relaxed yet alert. This is illustrated in Figure 17.2. Now you can see where the term 'flow state' comes from! This time the athlete was imagining a high-pressure competition having learned to apply the Three Foundations. This coherent state reinforces activity in the prefrontal lobes (cortical facilitation), enhancing their ability to think clearly and control the situation.

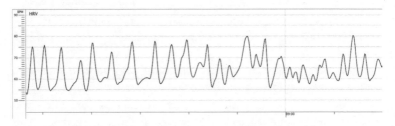

FIGURE 17.2 The heart rate variance (over 2–3 minutes) of the same athlete in a coherent state

Coherent states not only benefit your entire body, they also profoundly affect how you perceive, think, feel and perform. Therefore, the ability to create coherent states has proven itself to be an essential part of any high performer's mental preparation and training. Studies have demonstrated significantly improved reaction times, sustained attention, coordination and decision making among people who actively practise coherence techniques before performing a skilled task. Coherent states have also been shown to reduce performance anxiety and improve artistic performance in musicians.

Executives and business professionals trained to sustain coherence frequently report benefits such as a notable reduction in extraneous mental 'noise', increased clarity, more effective decision making, improved workflow, enhanced creativity, increased intuitive judgement and decreased rates of burnout. Several hospital studies have also shown a significant reduction in nursing staff turnover after they had been trained in coherence techniques.[2]

So now I hope you are ready to start practising for yourself!

The Three Foundations

The Three Foundations are simple in essence. I urge you to keep them simple but do them well. In fact, do them world-class. The challenge will not be in learning these Three Foundations; it will be in continuing to do them well as you start to layer in more pressure and stress in Phase 2.

Step 1: Breathing

Luckily, we've all been gifted with a simple and powerful tool for establishing and re-establishing coherent states no matter where we are or what we are doing. It's a tool so natural to us that it's easy to underappreciate the extent of its influence as we go about our busy lives. Despite the fact that this tool has the power to regulate your mood, regulate your mind, regulate your heart rhythms, regulate your biochemistry and even regulate the impact you have on people around you, we very often choose to ignore it. This tool is breathing.

I remember when I first studied the influence of breathing, my response was probably the same as yours: 'I've been breathing all my life – how much difference can this really make?' However, upon discovering how to regulate my breathing more effectively and then link it to my daily rituals and habits such as gym work, driving, preparing food and walking the dogs, I soon realised how much control I had lost by never giving myself time to focus on it properly.

Deep breathing needs to be incorporated into every aspect of a high-performance routine. It's your breathing that 'anchors' your physiology in any given moment, and your physiology then goes on to influence the quality of your thoughts, emotions and behaviours. Due to stress, incorrect habits and a sedentary lifestyle, we have forgotten how to breathe naturally and correctly. In particular, we are shallow breathing, using only a fifth or sixth of our lung capacity throughout the day. This has a hugely detrimental effect on mental and physical performance, not to mention our basic health and wellbeing.

Without wanting to overcomplicate matters, deep, rhythmical breathing is what we are looking for in this first foundation. The rhythm of your breathing directly controls the rhythm of your heart. Every breath in activates your sympathetic response and therefore allows your heart rate to increase, and every breath out stimulates your parasympathetic response, allowing the heart rate to decrease. Therefore your heart follows the rhythm of your breathing. Knowing this simple fact gives you direct access to your heart's rhythms and therefore indirect access to your mental, physiological and emotional state. There is no other tool for creating such a profound shift in your mind and body, and there is no other tool you really need. What's more, it is available to you 24/7 and is completely free.

There are many different breathing techniques out there, and many overlap in terms of their benefit. They all have three essential qualities: diaphragmatic, deep and rhythmical.

1 *Breathe from your diaphragm:* imagine your lungs are like huge triangles, they are much bigger at the bottom. To maximise your oxygen uptake focus on filling them from the bottom up. If it helps, rest your hand on your stomach, feeling it gently expand and contract with every breath.
2 *Breathe deeply:* ensure you fill your lungs by breathing all the way in and all the way out, but without forcing it.
3 *Breathe rhythmically:* ensure that you breathe in and out consistently by counting your breath. Typically, I would recommend in for a count of five and out for five. I have made some suggestions for how this can vary below.

Should I breathe in through my nose? In an ideal world, yes, because nasal breathing facilitates the relaxation (parasympathetic) response, therefore you should get used to nasal breathing whenever you can. However, if you are doing this as part of an active routine when your heart rate and breathing rate are elevated, it's more realistic to breathe in through the mouth, which is fine.

Breathing exercises

These are the most effective exercises to train your breathing:

- *Standard exercise*: sticking to the technique above, breathe in through your nose for a count of five and out through your mouth for a count of five. The counting will help you to maintain focus and regulate the flow and rhythm of each breath.
- *Slowing down when nervous or stressed*: extend the breath out, breathing in for five and out for seven (or whatever feels comfortable). The longer outbreath enhances your parasympathetic 'relaxation' response and therefore works well if you are particularly nervous or feeling stressed. When you are really nervous and try to breathe deeply, it may be impossible to breathe without stuttering. This is because you have been holding your breath and not using your diaphragm properly. You must keep working on taking deep, rhythmical breaths until you regain control.
- *Recovering your heart rate*: if you are physically active and trying to control your heart rate (e.g. during rests in an interval training session) I would recommend deep, even breaths. Start by breathing in and out for three counts, increasing to four or five as you recover your breath. Initially, you will need to breathe in through your mouth rather than your nose, that's not a problem, but remember it's essential to fill the lungs from the bottom. Speeding up your recovery is also reliant on muscular relaxation, which we will look at in the second foundation.

- *Energising*: this is very different from the other exercises and good for increasing your energy and alertness. Take a sharp intake of breath through your mouth, filling up your lungs from bottom to top, focusing on 'belly, chest, head' as you breathe in. On the out-breath, simply let go, allowing gravity to push the air out naturally without forcing it too much. This is a much more aggressive exercise than the others, but the principles of breathing deeply and rhythmically are still important. This might look and sound like hyperventilating, but it is not. Hyperventilation is reactive, shallow and uncontrolled. This technique is still controlled, deep and rhythmical. It will give you a surge of energy, but if you are new to it, don't do it for more than 10 breaths at a time.

The ultimate goal of breathing training is to make smooth, diaphragmatic breathing a 24-hour habit.

Now that you are breathing effectively, you can add the next layer of training coherent states: active relaxation.

Step 2: Active relaxation

Many people associate relaxation with putting their feet up at the end of a long day. But for high performers relaxation is a far more deliberate and active process that requires them to pay attention in order to do it properly.

With challenge comes intensity and with intensity comes energy. This energy is stored in the muscles, which means that, in the absence of being able to physically vent it (e.g. in an exam hall, standing on stage or sitting behind an office desk), it can quickly turn into tension if you don't train yourself to manage it.

To neatly highlight this problem, try getting a child to sit absolutely still while giving them some really exciting news. It's near impossible – instead, they want to run around and shout! Whether it comes from excitement or fear, this excess energy manifests itself as tension in the muscles. If you've ever experienced prolonged stress, excitement or anticipation in the build-up to an important event, you would have no doubt experienced 'creeping tension'. This is a build-up of muscular tension around the body over time.

Creeping tension

Just like with effective breathing, the first challenge with staying relaxed is that you tend to be unaware of creeping tension, so called because it can sneak up on you over days and weeks, especially in the run-up to a big event. For Sharon Hunt, Olympic bronze medallist in the sport of equestrian three-day eventing, this was an important realisation. Having applied these techniques to her training I remember her saying, 'I had no idea how tense I got until I learned how to stay actively relaxed.' This is something I have vivid memories of myself during my first World Cup competition in Budapest. Stuck on a bus on the way to the venue I decided to use the time to practise the relaxation techniques given to me by my own psychologist. Only when I started to focus inwardly on these techniques did I realise how tense I was. My legs in particular felt as hard as rock. It took 15 minutes of focused breathing and active relaxation before I could return them to a relaxed state. It scared me how something that could affect my performance so dramatically could escape my awareness. From that day onwards I started to take active relaxation practice far more seriously in my day-to-day training, much to the benefit of my results.

For athletes, muscular tension can have devastating consequences, affecting speed, rhythm, accuracy and longevity of their performance. But the truth is that *everyone's* performance suffers when muscular tension is allowed to take hold, not least because of the intrinsic link between muscular tension and mental tension. Learning how to sit with intensity while staying relaxed is an essential tool for reducing anxiety. Therefore, in conjunction with deep breathing, muscular relaxation is the first step towards nurturing a more composed, positive, responsive and creative mental state.

This makes active relaxation distinct from passive relaxation in so much as active relaxation requires you to concentrate on releasing tension. With enough practice you can teach your mind and body to notice low-level tension and respond positively to it before you are even consciously aware of it. This is a fundamental stepping stone towards converting bad stress into good stress, and your fight-or-flight response into your favoured 'challenge response'.

Active relaxation exercises

Once your breathing has settled into a consistent rhythm, practise this simple routine.

PROGRESSIVE RELAXATION

- The goal here is to link the sensation of relaxation to your breathing; therefore with every breath out focus on softening your muscles and releasing any tension.
- Focus on relaxing one area of the body at a time. You need to be able to tune your attention into specific muscle groups in order to learn how to control them.
- Your goal is to soften your muscles a little bit more with every breath you take.
- Start with your head, focus on releasing any tension in your forehead, around your eyes and through your jaw. Do this for as many breaths as you need to until the muscles stay relaxed.
- Now go around your body applying the same technique one area at a time – the neck and shoulders, arms and fingers, torso and hips, legs and feet.
- Take three breaths per area, more if you feel you need to.

ONE-BREATH RELAXATIONS

- Finish off with three one-breath relaxations. Do this by taking a really deep breath in, holding it for two seconds and then breathing all the way out while imagining a wave of relaxation running from the top of your head all the way down to the soles of your feet, releasing any tension out into the floor.

- Combine every out-breath with saying the word 'relax' or 'calm' to yourself. This will anchor the effect and allow you to achieve it more consistently when you start to apply it in response to stress in the next section.

This routine should take no longer than 5–10 minutes, and I recommend you do it twice a day. Over time you will become much more proficient as you are able to attain deeper levels of relaxation faster, but let it take as long as it takes.

Use the one-breath relaxation in response to any type of adrenaline rush, emotional spike or sudden onset of tension. Remember, you are trying to condition your mind and body to respond positively and consistently to any form of stress reaction.

Top tip

Yoga is a fantastic way of practising these techniques because it encourages you to hold quite challenging positions while simultaneously focusing on your breathing and relaxation. Only by relaxing more deeply can you expand your ability and develop control within the poses. This is as much a mental exercise as it is a physical one, opening up the line of communication between mind and body.

Step 3: Positive focus

Positive focus relates to visualising specific imagery which will help you to perform better. Done in conjunction with your breathing and relaxation, the goal is to link the images that you choose to focus on with the feeling of being in complete control. Over time you can start to do this with more challenging imagery and visualised skills. The idea is that you will need to work on maintaining your breathing and relaxation alongside increasingly challenging images (e.g. imagine an audience of 500 people rather than 50).

The words 'positive' and 'focus' are both important in their own right here. *Focus* relates to the ability to slow down your thoughts and narrow your attention. To do this you can use a simple image (e.g. a point in front of you to focus on, or a place where you have positive memories from your childhood). Alternatively, you can focus on a mantra or sound (there are many playlists that offer ambient sounds which are ideal). *Positive* relates to the quality of what you choose to focus on – it should be deliberate and meaningful. It should also evoke a positive and useful emotion such as calm, excitement, gratitude, challenge, pride and so forth – whatever you want to connect with the imagery.

While practising these Three Foundations, the most basic form of positive focus might simply start out as breathing and relaxation itself. If you are not well trained and practised, breathing and relaxation are themselves skills that require your full attention. The danger is that you try to focus on too much at once and you lose control of your other two foundations. It's strange to imagine that breathing and active relaxation are capable of occupying your full attention, but I've learned that when you want to do something world-class you must ensure that its component parts are also world-class. Chefs take the same attitude to their cuisine – they will tell you that a world-class dish starts with the quality of basic ingredients.

Once you have achieved good-quality breathing and relaxation as a basic parameter for controlled focus, you can start to layer in visualisation. In the Thinking Dimension we explored visualisation as a powerful tool for developing your skills, decision making and confidence. Visualisation is what allows you to practise your intent: priming and reinforcing the neural circuitry actually allows you to enact this intent with greater skill, precision and confidence.

Acclimatising yourself to a pressure environment

Before your mind will let you focus on the detail of an upcoming event, it must first feel comfortable with the environment. Sometimes just the very thought of being in a large stadium, on stage, in a combat zone or in an operating theatre may cause anxiety or distraction, in which case you must first acclimatise to these images. Visualisation therefore might start quite broadly before narrowing down to the specifics of your process or blueprint.

If you are not used to inviting challenging emotions in this way, you may be less willing to imagine these scenarios in advance. But that would make you far more vulnerable to a negative interpretation of the feelings that take hold when you arrive there. This very situation was highlighted to me in a rather wonderful way many years ago. I was working with an equestrian event rider. Eventing is effectively the triathlon of the equine world, consisting of the three disciplines of dressage, show jumping and cross-country. It's an exceptionally demanding sport that requires a huge range of skills and qualities from both horse and rider, as well as a very trusting relationship between them.

This particular rider was only weeks out from his first Olympics and was starting to visibly feel the pressure. He had never experienced a competition quite like this, with the world suddenly taking a keen interest. He played it down, but I could see it was getting to him. I got him to rehearse his full dressage test in his mind (which riders know and practise in advance), something he was used to doing, but this time I wanted him to do it while sitting on the horse.

Horses are very intuitive animals. Despite being domesticated, horses still behave as prey animals – they are extremely flighty and highly attuned to their surroundings. In equestrian sport, their willingness to perform is determined entirely by the leadership of the rider. If the rider is overly nervous and incoherent, they will unconsciously communicate this to the horse through tension and tiny deviations in the timing of their cues. It's also believed that horses have a sixth sense that allows them to pick up on the incoherence of other horses from across the herd, enabling them to respond to predators far more quickly than visual cues would allow them to. If they sense incoherence in the rider, the horse becomes visibly distracted, which then affects their performance as a partnership. For this reason I have often worked with business leaders using horses as a tool for honest feedback – horses don't tend to care if you are the CEO or the receptionist, they simply respond to how you make them feel.

In this case, something fascinating happened as the rider sat there on the horse, going through the competition in his mind. The horse started to shift impatiently on its feet, getting visibly fidgety. The rider, trying to concentrate on his task, was getting tense in the shoulders and his breathing pattern was becoming erratic. Within minutes the horse was moving so much, sensing the rider's tension, that the rider had to stop the exercise halfway through, remarking,

'I don't think I should be doing this on the horse.' No sooner had he said it he realised that this was the point. If by simply imagining the big day was enough to create tension in himself and his horse, imagine what would happen when he got there for real.

Every day for the final few weeks he practised visualising his test while consciously breathing deeply and staying relaxed, using his horse as feedback to tell him whether or not he was staying relaxed and coherent. They arrived together on the big day and managed to achieve their highest ever score.

Meditation and the Three Foundations

The use of meditation to improve health and performance is now widespread and continues to grow in popularity. Meanwhile, the benefits of meditative practice are now well documented in scientific journals.

Meditation and mindfulness are similar to the Three Foundations in terms of the core ingredients; however, meditation would never be presented in the same way in which I have presented the Three Foundations. This is because meditation is built upon an approach or philosophy rather than on a specific technique or activity – and this approach works very well in conjunction with the Three Foundations. Meditation focuses on a state of *being* rather than a state of *doing*. If you have learned to associate 'being busy' with 'making progress', the concept of meditation may not sit comfortably, let alone the practice itself. You may be more inclined to ask the question, 'What should I be doing?' when in fact meditation teaches you to ask, 'How do I want to be?' After all, we are human *beings*, not human *doings*.

This idea of 'being' as well as 'doing' is important in performance environments – gold medals can be won or lost in the anxious moments before a race, at the point where there is nothing to physically do. The reality of combat operations is that there is often far more waiting than there is doing. These are the times when negative feelings can surface, insecurities can swell and tension can mount. Very often, this is when important habits such as deep breathing are furthest from people's minds as they become consumed by the intensity of the situation they find themselves in. If you are able to apply mental training, you will be less affected by negative thoughts and anticipation while being better prepared to perform at your best.

In order to actually apply meditation to life, I think you have to get away from the popularised image of sitting cross-legged by a mountain lake or in a remote woodland retreat. These environments are lovely places to do it, but not an essential part of the meditation kit list. Ideally, meditation should allow us to function effectively in busy, noisy and even hostile environments. This is when you really need it. If you're thinking, 'the environment has to be right', then you're missing the point. That said, quiet, safe environments are perfect for learning these skills, in the same way that learning any skill is best done without distraction.

Therefore the Three Foundations offer an applied focus to the principles of meditation and mindfulness. For me, it was with my target shooting that I discovered this. I had got to a point where I started to realise that physical practice was no longer advancing my competition results. If anything, it was just reinforcing the idea that I was capable of shooting very well in training but struggled to perform to the same level when it really mattered in competition.

After a disastrous World Cup competition in Budapest where I fell apart, I knew I could no longer continue to train the way I was while expecting a different result. I decided that my poor results had nothing to do with my ability to shoot and everything to do with the state of mind I was in while shooting, something which I had never paid much attention to when training at home. On some level, I knew that my state of mind had to be practised on a daily basis if I was going to be able to recreate it with any degree of certainty in competition, but even with two degrees in psychology I wasn't sure exactly how to go about it.

One simple change would end up making a profound difference to my mental approach – and my results. I started to do much more dry firing (firing without actually loading the pistol). Only by doing this could I truly focus on my inner game, allowing me the freedom to practise without the distraction of results. Much of this I did in the kitchen at home – with a target pinned to the wall. I knew what a good shot felt like; therefore, if I was relying on the result to tell me, I was not reinforcing my own process, judgement and ultimately confidence from the Inside Out.

Breathing, relaxing and focusing became the central tenets of every shot, anchored to every part of my routine. I would raise the pistol to above the target while saying 'Calm' inside my head and taking a deep breath in. Then I lowered the pistol to the target while saying 'Control', and took a slow breath out, feeling my shoulders relax. Finally, I focused on the sights while saying to myself 'Sights' and squeezed the trigger. I was rehearsing exactly the same blueprint every time, first in my head and then with the pistol. For my brain, they pretty much merged into one. I was sometimes exhausted by the end of each session (simply because of the applied focus) but I was always clear-minded and some-what euphoric. I initially did this for 10 minutes, but after months of practice I was going for a full hour, my focus getting deeper and deeper.

Through this process I was carving out a groove in which my mind and body could apply themselves perfectly and consistently to this task. There's a phrase used by neurologists: 'What fires together wires together.' This means that you can train exactly the same pattern of breathing, heart rhythms, muscular relaxation, focus and action, all as one. Without this systemic approach, you merely focus on your actions and then wonder why the experience and outcome vary every time.

Your foundations are now stronger

This three-step coherence process not only can produce in-the-moment benefits but over time facilitate sustained changes in health, wellbeing and performance. The more these states are practised, the more they become increasingly familiar to the brain and body. These new, healthy patterns are thus reinforced and over time become established as a new baseline, which your whole system then automatically strives to maintain. The patterns that underlie the experience of stress are progressively replaced by healthier physiological, emotional, cognitive and behavioural patterns as the normal way of being.

There is also data linking coherence training to positive changes in hormonal patterns.[2] Research by the HeartMath Institute found that people who practised coherence techniques for 30 days demonstrated significant reductions in the stress hormone cortisol and significant increases in the hormone DHEA, which you may remember mediates our response to pressure. This finding has been interpreted as evidence of a repatterning process occurring at a fundamental level.

18
Phase 2: Expanding your comfort zone

Now that you can achieve coherent states at will, the next goal is to practise applying pressure. By maintaining a coherent state in an otherwise stressful situation, you are conditioning a very different response to pressure. This is called 'autonomic fitness' because you are effectively training your nervous system. You are teaching your mind and body to lead with your 'challenge response' rather than your fight-or-flight response. As we discovered earlier, this will generate dramatically different results. In this way, the Three Foundations start to bridge the Thinking Dimension and the Feeling Dimension, allowing your mental focus and routines (your blueprint) to be conditioned with a calm, relaxed physiological state.

On the morning of 3 June 2017, a rock climber named Alex Honnold took his first step on a journey that no one thought to be possible. He climbed up the vertical face of El Capitan in Yosemite National Park – 1,000 metres (3,280 ft) of sheer granite – without any rope, a pursuit known as free soloing. Many daring climbers have scaled great heights without ropes, but nothing like this had ever been attempted before, at least not without climbers plummeting to their death, as a number of Alex's friends had. Warren Harding first climbed the same route in 1958. It took him and his team 46 days over 16 months because they couldn't do it continuously. They were drilling bolts into the granite and pulling themselves up. In contrast, it took Alex 1 hour and 58 minutes – just him and the rock with zero margin for error.

Even with ropes this was not an easy climb. Scaling up the route there were a great number of highly technical pitches (a small section of the climb). In some places the edge of Alex's foot was in contact with only millimetres of rock. On one particular pitch he had to jump across the rock (460 m or 1,500 ft in the air) and grab on to a narrow ledge with just his fingers. His friend and fellow climber

Tommy Caldwell summed up the challenge in stark terms: there were only two outcomes here, win or die. That was the challenge Alex Honnold had given himself.

It would be easy to think that Alex had a death wish, that somehow he wasn't entirely sane, but Alex wasn't insane at all. He was completely aware of the scale of the challenge, and in the Oscar-winning film *Free Solo*, which documented his year-long preparation for the climb, it depicted Alex having many moments of doubt.

So how is a feat like this even possible? Well, there is no doubt that practising since the age of five would have helped Alex master some of the technical challenges, but being technically good doesn't necessarily prepare you emotionally for something as extreme as this. It's not enough to simply practise the route with ropes over and over again until you know you can do it without falling – and then take the ropes away. This is a logical approach, but the moment you take away the ropes, the challenge becomes a wholly different one. In the same way, imagine walking along the edge of a pavement. You wouldn't have any problem walking freely because there is no real danger. But now imagine the drop from the pavement wasn't three inches but three miles. How would you walk? Assuming you are not rooted to the spot, you would probably be very slow and cautious, probably wobbling and lacking any fluidity in your movement. The point here is that the challenge has nothing to do with your ability to walk. You haven't suddenly forgotten how to walk; therefore, it doesn't matter how much you step away from the edge to practise your walking, you are still not preparing yourself for the real challenge. That's because, once the technical skill is taken care of, the real challenge is an emotional one.

Therefore, technical ability aside, how did Alex train himself mentally for the sheer intensity of the climb? He built his own blueprint, or in his words a 'mental map', of the climb. This mapped out what the perfect climb would entail, including the precise route, the nature of each pitch and the precise techniques required to accomplish each pitch. But Alex acknowledged that this was only part of the visualised experience – this was the thinking and doing part. What he also needed was to understand the feeling part – what each pitch was going to *feel* like without a rope. He did this by practising a specific segment of the climb with a rope and asking the question: 'What would it be like to be here right now without a rope?' When he did this, you could see his expression visibly change as his mind and body responded to the visualised experience. You could see the fear taking a grip of him, his eyes on stalks and his body tightening up. He still had ropes, but he was inviting the fear so that he could practise working through it. Breathing, relaxing and noticing what options he would have available. He described this as 'expanding his comfort zone'. By adopting a proactive response to fear (i.e. inviting the scary feeling in a safe way rather than trying to suppress it) he was able to work through it and expand his zone of comfort. This is a great example of reappraising your emotions rather than suppressing them, which we highlighted earlier in our examples of surgery and Special Forces soldiers undergoing interrogation. For Alex, over the year he spent preparing, he was able to do this for each and every pitch, starting with the easier pitches and moving to the harder ones, until he knew that his emotions would no longer limit him.

This idea of expanding his comfort zone was reinforced by journaling. Alex would write down his observations in detail after every climb – not just his observations of the route and the technical solutions to each pitch, but also his observations of what was going on for him on the inside. 'Pitch 1: stay left towards the top, feels more secure. Pitch 2: trust right foot, rock-on, trust the feet ... Pitch 8: easy romp, go fast. Pitch 9: stay outside of the down climb. The key thing for the crux – pull hard, trust feet, TRUST!! – autopilot.' You can see from these journal entries how his inner game had to be just as explicit as his outer game. And interestingly, the word he uses most in his journal? Trust. Trust always seemed to be at the centre of being able to deal emotionally with a difficult pitch – trust in that foothold... trust in himself. If there was anything he didn't trust, he had to find a way to address that.

I hope you agree that this is a fascinating (albeit extreme) example of how to work with the Feeling Dimension. You may not be risking your life in pursuit of your goals but nonetheless the same principles apply to anyone with something to win and something to lose.

Alex's amazing story is a compelling example of working with fear and expanding your comfort zone. It reinforces the principle that you can actually condition a positive response to stress by simulating the challenging experience in your mind and coupling it with deep breathing, active relaxation and visualisation of the key skills required in that situation.

Train hard, fight easy

Positive adaptation requires controlled exposure to stress. This is a fundamental principle of psycho-physiological training. In order to strengthen your muscles and cardiovascular system you first have to apply significant stress to them. It is through this application of stress that they adapt to become stronger and more efficient. The technical term for this is super-compensation, and the effectiveness with which you adapt to become stronger and fitter is dependent on your work–rest ratios.

In weightlifting this involves stressing a muscle to the point at which its fibres literally start to break down. Given an optimum period of recovery, the muscle fibres will not only repair but repair stronger. Too much weight or too many repetitions without rest and the muscle will become over-damaged. Failure to stress the muscle enough and it will cause weakness and atrophy. Think about having your arm in a cast for six weeks – it re-emerges pale and thin. This is exactly the same for improving your mental resilience. You cannot get stronger by sheltering yourself from stress. Instead, you need controlled and systematic exposure to it. But in the same way that if you over-damage a muscle you may need to rest and recover slowly and incrementally, the same principle applies to mental training. If someone has had a particularly damaging experience and lost their confidence, then further stress can be damaging and they must build it back up again slowly, regardless of how much pressure they could tolerate beforehand.

To some extent, this idea of controlled exposure to stress is already integrated within military training and epitomised by the mantra 'Train hard, fight easy'. We would start by learning new skills and tactics in a relaxed classroom environment – effectively establishing our Thinking Dimension first. This would quickly progress to doing a 'walk-through, talk-through' on the parade square outside.

Bit by bit, the training would layer in new challenges: doing it at full speed, doing it sleep-deprived, doing it in the dark, doing it with live ammunition, and so on. Every time a new challenge was layered in, we would be at the limit of our ability and confidence, but never over. We had time before to plan and prepare, and time afterwards to debrief and make sense of what just happened. This was essential for converting intensity into confidence.

Similarly, if a team or organisation wants to apply this principle of applying controlled stress, individuals will adapt positively only if they start from a position of strength. Employees don't adapt positively by simply learning how to survive on the job, as many employers would like to think. Similar to the Special Forces replacing their mattresses on the Sennybridge Training Area, if you're going to deal in the currency of high intensity, you must back it up with clarity of mission and goals, quality planning, attention to wellbeing and social support.

The important point here is that stress, far from being the enemy, is actually the agent of growth and enhanced strength – but only when applied deliberately, in a controlled and systematic way, and when balanced with effective support and recovery.

With this as your objective, how else can you apply this concept to everyday life and in large organisations?

Stepping in and out of intensity

Practising A-Days

London's Heathrow is one of the largest airports in the world, with approximately 80 million passengers flying in and out every year. By far the largest operation within the airport is the security operation, employing over 4,500 staff to ensure the safety of every passenger. Head of this operation was Tom Willis, and in 2018 I was invited to go in and work with Tom and his team. I was soon educated in the sheer scale of the challenges they face on a daily basis and the relentless nature of keeping so many passengers safe and moving through the airport, not to mention protecting the 12.5 square kilometres (4.8 sq. miles) of real estate and the 71 kilometres (44 miles) of perimeter fencing.

In addition to safeguarding staff and passengers, the security team are responsible for ensuring the flow of footfall through the airport. Any unnecessary hold-ups create a backlog of passengers and queues that can quickly grow out of control. This then has a knock-on effect with boarding, plane standing times and, ultimately, departures. At an airport like Heathrow where one planes takes off or lands every 45 seconds, there is little tolerance for delay, and any delays that do occur are exceptionally difficult to claw back from.

When I was working with the security team, Heathrow was experiencing rapid growth. With passenger numbers increasing, peak days were becoming particularly problematic. The staff were well trained, having to stay focused and diligent from beginning to end of their shift while also offering a friendly customer experience for those passing through. But, on their feet all day, they found it difficult to maintain the intensity that this level of demand required. The moment intensity drops, problems occur. With a backlog of queues, problems to deal with and the pressure to keep people moving through the system, stress can accumulate easily.

Tom and his senior team identified this as a problem that was only going to grow alongside passenger numbers. At the same time they understood the importance of positive stress in keeping the team focused and effective during the busiest days of the year. Tom therefore developed a simple concept called 'A-Days'. These were special days designed to support and challenge the staff to raise their game in response to high demand. Airport numbers are highly predictable because they are based on airline bookings; therefore, the team were able to identify A-Days well in advance. Typically, this was when they were expecting in excess of 125,000 passengers going through departures in a single day.

A-Days were shaped by a blueprint that Tom and his team developed in order to maximise operational effectiveness. This consisted of procedures and protocols that would ensure everyone was aligned towards the same ultimate goal. For example, there would be no meetings or training allowed on an A-Day and all engineers would have to be able to get to the runway within 5 minutes rather than the normal 20 minutes. With hundreds of these small A-Day protocols in place, everyone was given the support they needed to rise to the challenge and give their very best. With A-Days clearly marked in everyone's diary, people were able to prepare mentally and physically for this challenge in advance. And they did.

Managers would plan days ahead with their teams, individuals were clear on their goals and priorities, team members would arrive with additional water and sustenance to keep everyone nourished throughout the day. People were even swapping their shoes for more practical ones that would offer them speed and comfort! Many of these small things had always been in their gift, but they had never been framed as part of a 'challenge'.

It was immediately clear to see how people arrived with positive energy to every A-Day. United in their challenge, all 4,500 members of staff expected to succeed. But even more significant was how they finished the day – with a smile on their face. In terms of performance, Tom reflected that, although they had endured many bad days at Heathrow, they had never had a bad A-Day. In fact, the metrics clearly showed that they very often performed at their best, despite peak passenger numbers.

We spoke earlier about the ability of high performers to steer their fight-or-flight response towards a 'challenge response' and in doing so to change their biology of resilience to shift from negative stress (distress), which is limiting, to positive stress (eustress), which is strengthening. This is a great example of how this can be achieved on an organisational scale.

You might be wondering why they couldn't just have an A-Day every day? Well, in this case there were practical implications, such as banning meetings, that would not be possible to do every day. But, that aside, there is another reason. High-performing behaviours are in themselves challenging to start and maintain, and at the centre of that is belief. Do you believe you can do it? Is it worth it? By concentrating your effort on a particular day or event, you learn what you are capable of when you fully apply yourself to your blueprint. This positive experience reinforces the new behaviours, which makes you more likely to want to do them again, but it takes time for these to become habit and therefore sustainable. By practising A-Days routinely, it will only be a matter time before A-Days move closer to normal days.

Stepping in and out of intensity is simply about being more deliberate in how you transition to and from pressure moments or periods.

Rather than being pushed around by pressure and allowing it to determine how they feel and behave, high performers instead dictate the terms upfront.

Creating thresholds

Another technique to help you step in and out of intensity more deliberately is about creating thresholds.

The Sports Training Village (STV) at the University of Bath is home to some of the UK's most successful Olympic sports. Athletes competing at the 2020 Tokyo Olympic Games returned with an incredible haul of 10 gold medals – an undeniable testament to the quality of training, coaching and support that they receive. A large and impressive building, the STV houses state-of-the-art facilities and spaces for athletes to train. Yet there are also two relatively unremarkable rooms in that building which, for me, play well to this idea of controlled intensity.

The first is the elite athletes' gym. This is an offshoot of the main gym, which is also open to members of the public. The elite athletes' gym was first installed by the England rugby team when they were using Bath as their training base. They needed to segregate the monstrous equipment which they brought with them, huge machines that hurt just to look at them. As a result, a glass partition was installed at one end of the main gym to create the two separate areas. When England Rugby eventually left, there was much talk about whether the glass wall should be left for the resident elite athletes or whether it should be taken down. Eventually, it was decided to leave it, but there would be specific rules for the athletes using it.

The glass wall dividing the two gyms has now become an important threshold. For a start, athletes are allowed inside only if they have a structured session written down, or if their strength and conditioning coach is with them to take them through the session. Phones are off limits (unless their sessions are written on them). Every exercise is done to the highest standard and with the greatest commitment. You start the session as soon as you arrive and you leave as soon as you have finished. There is no distracting anyone else doing their own session.

This raises the question: shouldn't professional athletes always be like that? Yes, in the same way that politicians should always be honest and teachers should care about the education of every one of their children. But we are human, and sometimes we respond well to prompts that help us to 'switch on'. High standards take huge effort. Just because you know something is the right thing doesn't mean you don't need plenty of encouragement along the way. Expecting athletes to maintain their A-game everyday on the basis that they are paid to do it is a deeply flawed argument, and one that can actually cause more damage than good.

For these athletes, what started as a conscious process, guided by clear rules and expectations, has become a much more intuitive one. From the moment they step through that glass door you can literally see them standing taller, breathing more deeply and narrowing their focus.

So what's the second room? Well, in contrast, the second room is a small, inconspicuous room tucked away to one side of the cafeteria. This is the athletes' recovery room. When I was there it was filled with beanbags and not much else. No coaches were allowed in this room, and generally people didn't tend to use technology in there. They mostly wanted to eat, chat and sleep. Remember, in order to train your 'on switch' you have to also train your 'off switch'.

Those who deal with intensity on a daily basis need to be just as deliberate about how they step out of this intensity, and if you can reinforce this in your environment, you stand a better chance of staying true to the standards you set yourself.

Fire in the heart, ice in the head – enhancing autonomic fitness

One form of controlled stress that's used commonly in sport is interval training. The idea is that, by repeatedly stressing the body with intense 'efforts' and then recovering between, your baseline fitness and tolerance for stress increase. Over time you will achieve the same physical results but with less physical effort. This is a principle used to enhance physical fitness, but it's also a principle I use to enhance mental fitness.

Earlier in the Feeling Dimension I shared the study I conducted with the modern pentathletes, getting them to conduct a shooting exercise (which required a high level of mental calm, focus and coordination) at increasing heart rates. Similar to this, the goal of mental fitness is to maintain a high level of coherence at increasing heart rates. This is the metaphorical equivalent of combining chess with boxing (a combination that I think was actually attempted in the United States). Hence 'fire in the heart, ice in the head'.

This is something I did with the GB skeleton team as part of their mental training. There are obvious benefits of keeping a clear head while under physical duress.

We started by simply using the Three Foundations to anchor a strong coherent state. The team were now well practised at this (using the techniques I described in Phase 1 earlier), so most of them could achieve strong coherence within a minute or two. For their positive focus they had to visualise standing at the top of the track in competition, ready to go. Naturally, this imagery evokes a degree of nervousness, but it's not long before the athletes are able to control this response using their foundation skills.

Sitting on a cycling machine, each athlete is connected to an HRV machine, allowing us to monitor their heart rate variance. Remember, we are looking for a strong wave pattern to indicate that they are coherent. Once they have been coherent for a few minutes, they start to cycle gently in order to raise their heart rate. They slowly increase their physical effort one level at a time (by turning up the resistance on the bike). As soon as they start to lose coherence they are instructed to hold their resistance and focus on maintaining the Three Foundations for a minute, after which they come back down to rest. This is repeated a number of times.

An alternative is to maximise the efforts as hard as you can for 30 seconds and then stop and rest for as long as it takes to regain coherence. The better your autonomic fitness, the quicker you return to coherence. This encourages you to focus on the recovery as much as the effort, which is essential because it's the mechanism of 'stress then release' that seems to be so important in training our autonomic fitness.

Over time, the athletes are conditioned to stay coherent at very high heart rates, giving them huge confidence to be able to achieve optimal performance states under high levels of physical and mental duress. Of course, we can amplify the challenge by introducing loud music and making it competitive, but no matter what is going on around them, success will always be about how they manage their internal state.

Chess prodigy Joshua Waitzkin used these very techniques to help him with his mental performance. In his book *The Art of Learning*, he remarked that it took just a couple of weeks to notice a clear improvement in his ability to relax and recover between the intense thought processes in a chess game and how, now, almost every aspect of his training incorporates some form of stress and recovery.

I think this raises an important question: do you have the physiological fitness to do a non-physical job? For me there is no doubt that physiological fitness enables our performance even in non-physical roles. It adapts our energy system to become more efficient, making more energy available to us over a longer period of time. Fitness promotes better-quality sleep, which has universal performance benefits. It also helps us to develop superior awareness of what's going on in our bodies, which is essential for managing optimal states of performance.

Interval training therefore becomes a great way of training your mental and physical range. By undertaking any activity that raises your heart rate in a controlled way, you have the opportunity to condition your Three Foundations as a positive response to stress.

But if interval training isn't your thing, there is another (increasingly popular) way you can develop your autonomic fitness.

Cold exposure – conditioning yourself to extremes

I'm lucky enough to live in the Cotswolds, a beautiful part of the English countryside. Outside my house is a narrow, meandering path that runs through the woods and down to a tranquil brook. Even on the coldest of winter mornings I like to run down there with my two cocker spaniels in tow, strip off and jump in.

The ice-cold water produces an instant shock to the system, a sudden awakening. Soon the adrenaline rush gives way to an almost euphoric feeling. No matter what my mood before I get in, I come out feeling charged and alive. What started off as a 30-second dip might now be anything up to 10 minutes, and in that time I concentrate on nothing other than deep breathing, relaxation and the nature around me. What I've learned is that your mind cannot afford to wander or else it inevitably gives way to the freezing sensation and with it a panic response, but by fixating on a point and maintaining a coherent state, my body stays calm, relaxed and, believe it or not, warm.

The effects are long-lasting, creating an energised afterglow that I'm conscious of for much of the morning. Ten years ago, this kind of behaviour might have got me arrested, but now it's considered normal among an ever-growing army of cold-water enthusiasts who have learned how to tap into nature's abundant energy. It sounds extreme, but the effects on your mind and body can be profound, as science is starting to understand.

The benefits of such behaviours have long been reported anecdotally and celebrated in mass events such as the famous New Year's Day swim in the icy North Sea off the coast of Scotland. In recent years cold tolerance has been taken to new levels by a Dutch guru, Wim Hof, also known as the Ice Man. Wim Hof has broken 20 world records related to cold exposure. He is capable of extraordinary things, such as standing in a container filled with ice cubes for two hours, climbing Mount Kilimanjaro in shorts, running marathons around the polar circle and swimming 200 metres (656 ft) underwater in the Arctic. These are feats that previously had been considered scientifically impossible.

In recent years, scientists have been eager to find out exactly what's going on here and whether we can all benefit from this style of mind–body training. Controlled experiments have now uncovered some of the mechanisms that sit behind this extraordinary ability and the psycho-physiological techniques used to achieve it.

For me, the most ground-breaking of these studies was conducted in 2011 at Radboud University in the Netherlands.[1] This was the first study to show that, through a combination of breathing techniques, focus and cold exposure, Wim was able to voluntarily influence his autonomic nervous system. Until this point this was something the medical community had thought impossible. This discovery has major consequences for human performance and the interaction between mind and body, not just for those seeking enhanced performance but also for the healthcare industry as a whole.

Frequent exposure to cold is linked to a number of health benefits. For example, it's been known for some time that ice baths speed up recovery after physical exercise as well as enhancing metabolism and reducing inflammation. For this reason, they are a staple part of any athlete's routine. But now we are learning that this is potentially just the tip of the iceberg, so to speak. There is growing evidence that we may all benefit significantly from such practices – mentally and not just physically – thanks to increasing evidence that gradual, controlled exposure to cold could transform our response to stress, thereby enhancing essential functions such as energy production, focus, quality of sleep and even our immune response to disease. In doing so it may even have an indirect impact on symptoms of mental wellbeing such as anxiety and depression.

The extent of all the scientific discoveries in relation to cold exposure is remarkable and mostly beyond the remit of this book, so I want to focus on the elements that add to our narrative of Inside Out, and in particular our ability to control our autonomic nervous system in response to stress. This is a skill that would be profoundly valuable to all of us, since it would allow us to exercise more control over some of life's most challenging situations. Importantly, the goal here is not to walk to the North Pole naked (unless you want to). The goal is to train our challenge response to acute stress and in doing so strengthen our mental and physiological resilience.

How to practise cold water exposure

Cold water training is another way in which you can practise your Three Foundations: deep breathing, active relaxation and positive focus. The only difference now is that you are layering in an extreme stress response in the form of cold water which will test your ability to maintain a deep, rhythmical breathing pattern alongside muscular relaxation.

The research to date shows that it's the interaction of these components that appears to activate positive adaptation. Coherent states have the capacity to override your primitive fight-or-flight response, allowing your body to regulate its temperature effectively in the icy conditions. Here you are reconditioning your response to the sensory signals arriving from around the body, up through the brain stem and into the limbic system. For Wim Hof, this allowed him to maintain a normal temperature for 80 minutes in an ice chamber where scientists believed the body should drop in temperature after 3 minutes. This was impressive and extremely beneficial for scientific research, but you don't need to go to this extreme to get the amazing benefits.

As an essential starting point, cold exposure should be very gradual over time. If you are pregnant or have any medical concerns such as a known heart condition, definitely seek advice from your doctor beforehand. You don't need to make it too extreme to derive positive effects. Don't worry if you don't have a glacial lake nearby or a bath full of ice. Cold showers a few times a week can have the desired effect.

It's very important to remember that you are training yourself to stay in control in spite of your body's natural shock response. The moment you enter cold water, you will feel a surge of energy. It's important that your very first response is to relax and stay focused on breathing deeply. Practise this for a few minutes before getting in so that your mind and body are already in the correct state and not trying to 'catch up'. You might feel the cold in waves and as a result your concentration may waver, but as long as you come back to your deep breathing and active relaxation, you will feel yourself starting to settle. Pick an object in the room or a point on the wall to focus on. Together with your breathing, this helps you to maintain blood flow to your frontal lobes, thus avoiding an emotional hijack.

It is not a competition to see how long you can last – seriously. This would defeat the object. The whole point is that the experience is non-forced – in other words, you are relaxing into the experience, not fighting it. When you see people enduring the cold with gritted teeth, screaming and shouting, they are just reinforcing their shock response and therefore doing themselves no good. It is not about fighting or resisting it – quite the opposite. You are training yourself to relax into it. As long as you remain coherent, your body will respond accordingly.

Remember that adaptation over time is both a mental and a physical process. Even if you maintain the relaxed concentration of a Zen master, your physiological processes still need to be trained to the experience. Therefore make sure you progress slowly – from 30 seconds to 1 minute, to 2 minutes, to 5 minutes over a month or so. The main thing is that you maintain your breathing, your relaxation and your positive focus.

Relish the intensity

Whether taking a dip in an icy pool is for you or not, it's the principle of controlled exposure to stress that's important when it comes to expanding your comfort zone and training your autonomic fitness, and this can be done in many different ways.

In the Feeling Dimension you've learned how to manage the emotional and physiological intensity of high performance. You've done this by reframing your relationship with nerves and stress while recognising the importance of recovery. You have also explored the importance of emotions in high performance, how to tune into them and how to reappraise them. Finally, you have learned how to establish coherent states of mind and body, as well as how to maintain these coherent states as stress increases.

If nothing else, I hope this dimension helps you to realise that you have more choice in how you manage your performance state than you may have realised. Essentially, these techniques and principles are all designed to help you 'lean in' to challenge rather than 'lean away' from it. Faced with any difficulty, you choose your attitude: you choose to be prepared or hopeful, sad or grateful, scared or excited, relaxed or tense. And it's how confident you are in enacting these choices that seems to determine how your physical body responds.

As a society we largely fail to frame stress as potentially enhancing, often missing opportunities to learn from and grow from stressful moments. Not all stress is positive, but by embracing your challenge response as a powerful tool for helping you overcome the inevitable challenges in life, you may discover opportunity and growth in the places you least expect.

Next up we delve into your unconscious as we explore the most fascinating and mysterious dimension, the Intuitive Dimension. Here you will discover how much you rely on your 'sixth sense' to perform at your very best. You will learn how to better listen to your intuition and build your intuitive 'library', and you'll finish by mastering the most elusive state of peak performance – flow state.

PART 3
The Intuitive Dimension

Pyeongchang, 2018

'Lizzy Yarnold's greatest strength is her intuition.' I heard this on many occasions from her coaches. In speed sports like skeleton where you travel up to 145 kilometres per hour (90 mph) head first with no brakes, intuition is a good friend to have. Among other things it allows for unconscious decisions and corrections to be made well before your conscious mind is even aware. When you lose access to this intuition, the impact on your performance can be significant.

Having taken a break after the Sochi Olympics, Lizzy came back to the sport two years before the 2018 Winter Olympics in South Korea with one goal in mind – to become the first Briton in history to defend a gold medal at the Winter Olympics. Because she had been so dominant in the sport, many people believed this would be a matter of course. I don't think anyone – including Lizzy herself – realised how tough it was going to be for her to re-establish herself as the world's best. The year prior to the Pyeongchang Winter Games reminded me of one very important truth in any high-performance arena: the greatest challenge isn't getting to the top, it's staying at the top.

On Lizzy's return, things were different. When you leave top-level sport for even the shortest amount of time, everything moves on: the skills, the technology, the coaching, the competition. Even the relationship Lizzy had with her teammates had moved on. They were all coming from a different place – Lizzy had achieved the dream in

Sochi and everyone was now hungry to do the same. In these circumstances it's easy to feel isolated. The irony is you are surrounded by more people than you ever have been – admiring audiences at public events, friends wanting to share your success, agents, media, followers on social media – and yet it's not uncommon to feel more isolated than ever. You often hear the same sentiments from CEOs and celebrities – and I'm sure you would from politicians, if they were allowed to admit it.

If you are relatively ruthless and goal-focused, this shift might not be too difficult to deal with. But for a caring, person-centred character like Lizzy, a close and equal relationship with her team is important – it is her base camp that gives her the resilience to go through discomfort on the mountain. This is the paradox of reaching the top of your game – a huge part of your success is down to the connection you have with a bunch of very committed and talented people close to your performance. On the way up you are given the support, the challenge, the care, the guidance and the encouragement – basically everything you need to thrive. But when you've reached the top, people treat you differently. They don't mean to, and they generally have your best interests at heart, but inside they're thinking, 'She's got this – she's the world number one.' People get on with their jobs, expecting you to deliver.

This extends to the competitive world which also never stands still. When you have dominated your field to the extent that Lizzy had, people study you closely, looking for anything they can learn and improve in their own performance. There is no element of surprise any more. Every time you raise the bar it simply inspires your competitors to do the same, fuelling their desire to achieve more.

When Lizzy finally returned to competition no one expected her results to be back to where they were two years earlier, but likewise no one was expecting her to finish consistently outside the top 15. Lizzy was struggling to rediscover her form: lacking the sharpness and intuition she was so well known for, people questioned whether she still had it in her. With just one year to go until the Pyeongchang Olympics, her hopes of being the first British athlete in history to become a double Winter Olympic champion were dealt another huge blow with a succession of physical injuries, including crippling back pain and a worsening vestibular condition that had triggered blackouts when travelling at peak speeds down the mountain. Yet Lizzy battled on. The problem is that fighting for survival is unlikely to lead to optimal performance, and Lizzy didn't have long left to turn things around. She would have only three months of competition to rediscover her form from four years earlier.

Olympic season didn't start well – her performances, if anything, slid backwards. To make matters worse, her vestibular issues were getting more severe – and she was becoming frightened. With confidence waning, pressure was mounting. There was still an overriding sense that she had it in her, but everyone's blind faith did little to comfort her at this time. Lizzy found herself scrambling for answers, placing huge hope on small technical changes on the track and in the gym – anything that would help her find the path back to where she had been. It was a challenging time and something needed to change.

Times like this are just as difficult for an athlete's support team, who also feel partly responsible when things aren't going well. It's easy to clutch at straws yourself, deviating from established processes and potentially confusing the athlete at critical times. The best thing you can do is to detach yourself from the emotion of it all and encourage the truth to be spoken. There were now just two competitions left before the Olympics, and if nothing changed Lizzy would be relying on pure luck to have any hope of achieving her dream. But luck didn't feel like a good currency to invest in, and it certainly wasn't Lizzy's style.

So what was the truth that had to be spoken? What were the assumptions and patterns of thinking that were obstructing her ability to access what she knew she had inside her? The first one was the story being told to the outside world. Athletes tend to feel the pressure to report that everything is going to plan – everything's fine – even when it's not. When it comes to sports like skeleton, most media platforms show a disproportionate interest once every four years around the Olympics, which for the athlete amplifies the presence of journalists when they show up. You get used to sharing the same story over and over again, and to the outside world it was a great story – Lizzy was on course to become the first Briton to win back-to-back Olympics. Except she wasn't – at the time she wasn't even close. But as long as this was the story being told, there would be a layer of untruth that Lizzy would have to suppress. You may remember from the Thinking Dimension what happens when your mind is working in the background to suppress unhelpful or difficult thoughts – it becomes tiring, it creates incongruence and ultimately your mental performance pays a price.

In this case the brutal truth was that Lizzy was not favourite to win. More than that, she wasn't even the best British athlete – Laura Deas had been outperforming her for some time. I imagine it took huge courage to admit this, but by saying it out loud it opened up the opportunity to change the narrative – to create a new story that Lizzy could actually believe in. This was a turning point, and it had nothing to do with fitness, technique or strategy; rather, it was about acceptance and letting go of an unhelpful burden. This would create at least a little space for her – freedom to move. At the same time Lizzy looked back over her old training diaries pre-dating the Olympics in Sochi to see whether there was any indication of what was different. The disparity was significant. Her old notes were far more detailed and the language was precise and even creative. It reflected how she wanted every corner to feel as well as the cues for doing it. They were far more convincing than the notes she was currently writing, which were vague and uninspired. They lacked the precision of language and the 'feel' that was so important to how she learned the track. What used to be an immersive experience with a clear sense of 'why' for every decision she made had become a robotic process, going through the motions. As she later described it, she hadn't been 'connected' to her performance in any meaningful way and as a result her intuition had been stifled. This highlighted a number of related challenges which she was able to address with her team going into the final two competitions before the Olympics. She didn't have long left, but, as everyone was still saying, if she could just reconnect with her intuition, she could do anything on the day.

For the first time in a while Lizzy was able to anchor her focus on meaningful goals – goals that she knew she could control and goals which she genuinely believed would make a difference. Her track walks were essential, finding the right cues and visualising every corner to pinpoint precision. This allowed her to plan with confidence and communicate with her team in the assured manner she had once enjoyed. The goal was simple: commit to the process wholeheartedly and let the result take care of itself.

In her final two competitions before the Pyeongchang Olympics she finished ninth and fourth – her best results for some time. She knew the plan was working, she just had to stay committed to it. But the build-up to the big race still had some twists and turns in store for Lizzy.

Days before her Olympic race Lizzy started to feel ill. She felt worse as the days and hours ticked by. Lizzy would later learn that she had been suffering with a severe chest infection which was made considerably worse by the intense cold, dust in the air and, of course, the brutality of the sport itself.

In the first run of four she held it together but felt dizzy at the end. She hadn't been breathing down the run (athletes normally take sharp intakes of breath). She finished the run visibly disoriented, faint and out of breath. Lizzy feared she wouldn't be able to continue. In the one hour between run one and run two she tried phoning her family. Eventually, she got through to her husband, James, and told him she didn't think she could go again – she couldn't see or walk properly. However, after receiving advice from the team she decided she would continue, but she was genuinely scared for her safety. Her final words to Louise, her physio, before her second run were, 'If I slide, could it kill me?' Louise's response was critical. 'No, just remember to breathe.' Lizzy got through the second run as the ninth quickest, leaving her in third place overall at the halfway point.

That night Lizzy didn't get much sleep. Her body was in turmoil, she was struggling to breathe and she had to sleep upright. Nonetheless she focused on what she could control, keeping relaxed and optimistic. She had got this far, and for the first time she thought it might be possible. Despite all that had happened to her, she was rediscovering her best self.

Lizzy woke up the next morning cutting the same shape as the person who won gold in Sochi – for the first time since Sochi. In her next run she laid down a solid performance that took her back up to second place with one run to go. Lizzy had the bit between her teeth, and it was on this final run that she delivered an almost perfect run – smashing the track record to win her second gold medal and become the first person in British Winter Olympic history to do so. Her story had come true.

It turns out that her coaches had been right – her greatest strength was her intuition and on that fateful day she managed to rediscover it.

19
Intuition: being guided by your subconscious

Intuition is a mind–body intelligence, integrating how you feel with how you think. It allows you to perceive a situation with the collective wisdom of all your senses and all your experiences coming together. This convergence creates what some might call our sixth sense. Unsurprisingly, this becomes a powerful tool in any performance environment where we have limited time to work things out consciously.

We all have this sixth sense and we are all dependent on it to live and operate effectively; however, we often don't make the most of it because we either don't develop it properly in the first place or we smother it by not listening to it. In the arena of high performance, intuition very often differentiates the good from the great.

One thing is important to clarify from the outset, which is that intuition is not the same as instinct. Instinct tends to refer to what we are born with and is actually quite limited. For example, we are born with an inbuilt fear of falling, loud noises and some specific visual cues (such as snakes). Our reactions to these stimuli are instinctive – we all have them to one degree or another. Intuition, meanwhile, has to be nurtured. The illusion of being born with inbuilt talents is a compelling one, not least because rudimentary skills that set apart one child from another can be expressed at a very young age. An acorn has the potential to grow into an oak tree, but it's still just an acorn – it needs a sustained nurturing environment for this potential to be realised. Intuition may be helped along by some favourable traits (such as numerical reasoning for an accountant), but it still has to be honed through many hours of practice. It's these hours of deliberate practice that create the 'library' of experience that your intuition needs in order to work well for you.

Like the other dimensions, the Intuitive Dimension is one you can develop in equal measure, regardless of your starting point. This leads us to ask two key questions about our Intuitive Dimension: 1) How am I responsible for training and shaping my intuition? 2) How do I access it when I need it?

The power of your subconscious

In a study at the University of Iowa, gamblers were asked to play a card game where they pulled cards from two different decks. The decks were rigged so that one would 'win' more often than the other, but the participants didn't know that. It took about 50 cards for participants to consciously realise that the decks were different and about 80 cards for them to figure out what that difference was.

That much is straightforward – the conscious mind needs enough experience of turning over the cards to be able to pick up on a pattern. However, what the scientists had also done was connect the gamblers with a device that measured sweat on the palm of their hand, an accurate way of measuring micro-stress responses. It took only about 10 cards for them to start registering a response on the device – every time they reached for the 'losing' deck. This happened to be about the same time that they started to subconsciously favour the 'winning' deck.

This study has been replicated in many other contexts and reinforces the ability of our subconscious intuition to establish meaningful patterns from minimal information. Having observed this for many years in highly skilled professionals from all performance arenas, it's my belief that the Intuitive Dimension is one of the most powerful forces in human performance, and yet it's the one we understand the least. Why? Because it's extremely hard to measure and monitor objectively. We can monitor our thoughts, decisions, feelings and actions relatively easily, but what gives the Intuitive Dimension its air of mystery is that it operates below the radar, within the realms of our subconscious mind.

If you were to represent the mind by a large sheet of flip chart paper, many psychologists would agree that the conscious part of the mind would be represented by a small dot in the middle. Whether you like this idea or not, your conscious experience of the world is tiny compared with the work that is going on underneath the surface. These subconscious processes (mental and physical) tend to present themselves in the form of intuition, giving you a 'feel' for a situation and what to do. The goal of the Intuitive Dimension is to ensure that this information presents itself in a way that is helpful to your performance rather than a hindrance.

It's important to understand here the difference between what many believe to be the same – your *un*conscious and your *sub*conscious. Your unconscious refers to 'deep' processes going on inside you that happen automatically and cannot be brought to your conscious attention. By contrast, your subconscious is anything happening in the background that you can choose to bring to your conscious awareness if you actively focus your attention on it. For example, imagine your excitement at bumping into an old friend you haven't seen for years. Without realising it, your reaction will be governed by your past associations and interactions with this person. You are not thinking consciously about these past interactions, but if you wanted to bring them all to mind in order to understand why you feel excited, you could. Clearly, in the moment this is not your concern; instead you simply accept your sense of joy and allow yourself to behave accordingly by throwing your arms around them.

A good analogy is to think of your conscious as being like your focused vision and your subconscious as being like your peripheral vision. Whereas you can focus your eyes on only one area at a time, there is a wealth of information in your peripheral vision that your brain is still capable of processing – just not consciously. If, however, you choose to broaden your focus and notice what's going on in your peripheral vision, then you can.

For the sake of simplicity, in this book I will refer to any nonconscious processes as subconscious.

You still have responsibility for the mind you can't see

The scale and power of the subconscious mind do not diminish the importance and influence of the conscious mind. Imagine the CEO of a vast global company with more than 50,000 employees, where the CEO represents the conscious mind and the business (along with everything that happens within it) represents the subconscious mind.

The CEO cannot possibly process the tiny details of everything and everyone in that business, from the thousands of emails being sent 24 hours a day to the intricate network of relationships being formed and the maintenance of infrastructure like buildings and technology. On this level, the CEO knows very little, and if she tried to understand her business on this level she may get overwhelmed. Instead, her job is to make important decisions for the business. To do this, she needs an effective filter, with people and processes ensuring she gets the right information and support at the right time. This will be influenced by her vision for the business – different goals will make different information important to her. In turn, the decisions she makes will impact the lives and behaviours of thousands of people she may never meet. So, yes, she is only one of 50,000 people in the business, but she has an essential role to play in interpreting and guiding the system. In the same way, your conscious mind may be dwarfed by the scale of subconscious processes happening beneath the surface, but it still plays an essential role in how these subconscious processes are expressed.

This analogy illustrates four important lessons for how you get the most from your subconscious mind and the intuition that comes from it:

1 If you ignore your intuition, you cannot tap into the extensive wisdom that comes from your subconscious.
2 Your intuition will support you well if you listen to it, nurture it and provide it with the experience it needs to make better judgements.
3 You can help your intuition work better for you when you are clear in your vision, your goals and your intents.

Intuition boils down to the brain's ability to match patterns, something it can do better than any supercomputer known to humanity. These intuitive patterns can be mental (affecting the way you solve problems and make decisions) or physical (affecting the way your skills become automated – doing without thinking). Equally impressive is the phenomenal speed with which your mind can process these patterns.

Whereas conscious thought has a linear logic to it (I must go from A to B to get to C), intuition is more like a black box – in goes a situation and out comes … a hunch, a gut feeling. Hardly any wonder you don't always trust what comes out, but the more you understand your intuition, the more you will be able to tune into it and operate at a higher level of performance.

Benefits of intuition for your performance

Applied well, our Intuitive Dimension has three distinct advantages: speed, efficiency and accuracy. These can come together with devastating effect.

Conscious thought is incredibly energy-consuming. The brain accounts for just 2 per cent of your body weight yet it uses 20 per cent of the body's energy resources to function and most of this energy goes into paying conscious attention to the world around you. Your intuitive 'autopilot', meanwhile, is much quicker and is hyper-efficient. It uses only a fraction of this energy, despite being hugely influential in most of your behaviour. It does this by creating efficient pathways in the form of habits that require no conscious input from you. Due to the efficiency of these pathways, which effectively act as mental shortcuts, your intuitive judgement is much faster than your conscious judgement. Perhaps more surprisingly, it tends to be more accurate as well. In one study, car buyers who relied on careful analysis of all the available information were happy with their purchases about 25 per cent of the time, while buyers who made quicker, more intuitive purchases were happy 60 per cent of the time.

But how are these intuitive feelings and judgements formed? They don't just materialise from nowhere and present themselves to your conscious. In this way a writer can't simply sit down and expect inspiration to come from nothing. Instead, he must guide his attention towards cues that evoke feelings, thoughts and memories that open up new patterns in his mind.

A wonderful example of this comes from the Robert Pirsig's philosophical book *Zen and the Art of Motorcycle Maintenance*.[1] The main character, Phaedrus, is teaching a young student who is suffering a mental block trying to write a 500-word story about her hometown. The student was struggling to get beyond the idea that her town was small and boring and there was nothing particularly interesting to write about. She couldn't write a word. Phaedrus, a brilliant and eccentric man, decided to change the assignment, and in doing so liberated the girl from her writer's block. He asked her to write about the front of the theatre outside her classroom, situated on a small street in a small neighbourhood of that dull town. He suggested she begin with the upper left-hand brick. At first, she was incredulous, but then a flow of creativity ensued and she couldn't stop writing.

This is an essential principle of performance psychology and one I use a lot with clients. By helping them to shift their conscious attention towards something detailed but simple and compelling within their ability and control, it starts to open up a network of complementary feelings and skills which seamlessly flow together in high-definition and Technicolor. It can be like someone discovering a valuable part of themselves they never realised they had.

Intuitive states of mind

Being in the right state of mind is an essential ingredient for accessing your intuition. If, for example, you are incoherent, anxious or rushed, you will detract from the conditions required in the brain for intuition to work effectively. The conscious mind is a potent tool, but it's slow and can process only a small amount of information at once. The subconscious, meanwhile, is far more efficient. It processes significantly more data in much shorter time frames. Therefore, in peak performance states, the subconscious mind largely runs the show. As this occurs, a number of performance-enhancing neuro-chemicals flood the system, including noradrenaline and dopamine. Both of these chemicals amplify focus, muscle reaction times and pattern recognition. With the subconscious in charge and these neurochemicals in play you can access a level of performance you wouldn't otherwise have. You have the mental space and acuity to pick up tiny details. These details may not be processed consciously, but rather acted upon subconsciously.

Therefore, achieving flow states is a highly desirable part of the Intuitive Dimension and an area we will explore in more detail later.

20

Judgement: training and listening to your intuition

Intuition is important to all of us, but in some professions it's not just a nice-to-have, it's essential. Back in the Thinking Dimension you might remember meeting fighter pilot Luke O'Sullivan. There can't be many activities more taxing for mind and body than flying an F18 (Super Hornet) in air-to-air combat. With only so much that the conscious mind can process and control in the moment, Luke is reliant on his trained subconscious in order to deal with the mental and physical demands of the job. But how does this trained subconscious actually present itself?

Luke describes how one of the most hair-raising parts of flying an F18 is actually landing it on the back of an aircraft carrier in the middle of the ocean. With such a small strip of runway to aim for, there is almost no margin for error. A large hook on the back of the aircraft catches a wire that's fixed to the deck of the carrier, bringing the plane to a swift stop. If you get the landing wrong and the hook misses the wire, you must react sharply to re-engage the thrust and get back up in the air (a process called a 'bolter'). Unsurprisingly, this can be a scary experience when the margins are so fine – you are never that far away from the edge of the deck. Every landing is intense, requiring total focus and concentration. Flying towards the deck at the right speed and angle is essential. It's tempting to try to overcontrol it and lose smoothness, so it becomes a delicate dance between conscious and subconscious judgement. Luke describes the moment when the hairs on the back of his neck might suddenly stand up, causing him to adjust the plane without knowing why. Moments later he realises that his closure rate (his speed of approach towards the carrier) is too fast. Remarkably, his subconscious mind knew to adjust the plane well before his conscious. This demonstrates how his subconscious is capable of speaking to his body, telling his muscles exactly how to react – a bit like a reflex.

This is a powerful example of how your trained subconscious makes itself known. It's also a good example of why you must learn to trust your trained intuition rather than second-guess it. It's easy to get in its way.

So what's going on in your brain and body to have this effect? Intuition starts in the right hemisphere of your brain's cerebral cortex, the same area that responds to music and other creative arts. While the left-hand side of the brain is associated more with verbal reasoning and logic, the right hemisphere likes to play with patterns. As you take in details about a situation or person, your right brain immediately holds up the emerging picture against your earlier experiences. It's asking, 'What's the story here?' as it looks for similarities and differences to events from your past. These conclusions are sent directly to your hormonal system, your muscles and your gut – preparing you to act. The precise balance of these messages gives rise to nuanced sensations, which are your first conscious awareness that something is up.

In other words, your intuition presents itself to you not in logical terms but in emotional terms. You feel pleased, worried, expectant or wary – without being able to tell why. It is quite literally a gut sense that something is right or wrong. When you tell someone to trust their gut, you are actually telling them to trust the conclusions of their brain's supercomputer, which is speaking to their gut. Try to acknowledge and attune yourself to these subtle, fleeting feelings of intuition. Monitor them and be curious. You don't always need to act on them, just don't ignore them.

From this point the best thing you can do is to use your judgement to evaluate what your gut is telling you before deciding how to act. For example, if you are about to jump out of an aeroplane for the first time, you are likely to get a strong gut feeling. You may interpret this gut feeling to be encouraging you not to do it. But your better judgement knows that, without a reasonable reference point for having done it before, this is going to be your natural fear response. Therefore, it's okay to politely ignore it. Better still, apply what you learned in the Feeling Dimension and interpret the feeling as excitement, saying out loud: 'I am excited! I am excited! I am excited!' By your fifth parachute jump your right brain will have a new pattern of experience to match against future jumps.

Despite reaching a high level of intuition, Luke is very mindful about routinely going back to 'training mode'. For him this often involves flight simulators where he can press pause and process information in slow time. This allows him to break his thought process and responses back down, going through the manual 'workings out'. This systematic activity rebuilds a more refined version of the processes that take place subconsciously. It also screens for any bad habits that may have crept in, such as focusing on the wrong visual cues. This process of reconnecting with the basics is easy to ignore once you get to a high level of competence, but in order to progress further at this point it's an important part of the process. Try to go back and refine your own world-class basics routinely; they are essential foundations to your intuition.

Priming your subconscious

As well as training your intuition through experience, it's important to know how to 'prime' it. A group of Dutch researchers did a study in which they got participants to answer 42 fairly demanding questions from the board game *Trivial Pursuit*.[1] Half were asked to take five minutes beforehand to think about what it meant to be a professor and to write down everything that came to mind. The other half were asked to think about what it meant to be a soccer hooligan. Those students who imagined the professor got 55.6 per cent of the questions right, whereas those who imagined being the hooligan answered only 42.6 per cent correctly. Statistically, this was a huge difference in scores – but why? How? The professor group didn't know more than the soccer hooligan group and they weren't smarter or more focused. They were simply in a smart frame of mind.

This demonstrates the power of priming your brain for optimal function. Based on a phenomenon called 'state congruence', your behaviour and performance are matched by the representation you have of yourself at that point in time. In this case, imagining a professor is enough to flick the switch on all subconscious associations with professors, including their behaviours and the way they think. This helps you perform like a professor – quite literally.

It's important to note that this priming effect helps you to access the intuition and deep knowledge you already have, but it can't help you pluck knowledge from thin air. The group associating with hooligans were primed with a very different state, activating an intuitive system far less congruent with a game like *Trivial Pursuit*.

This principle of priming your subconscious is one I commonly use in my coaching. By getting an athlete, for example, to imagine they were in the mind and body of someone they really admire (or indeed the best version of themselves), I get them to walk through various challenging scenarios while experiencing the decisions they would make and the fluidity with which they would respond and perform. This is one of the active ingredients of visualisation. If you imagine yourself executing on specific goals and being the athlete you want to be, you create the internal conditions that make that reality more likely, not simply by priming your conscious thoughts and actions but also by priming your subconscious.

Intuition needs structure

Regardless of how good you are at tuning into your intuition, it is only as powerful as the library of experiences it can call upon.

Imagine all the knowledge and experience you have ever amassed in life being stored in a cavernous library within your subconscious mind. The bigger the library, the more informed your intuition can be. But no matter how much information resides within this space, it's only helpful to you if you have a way of accessing it. This is where real libraries need complex indexing systems that can direct you to the right room, the right row, the right shelf and the precise location of the book you are looking for as quickly as possible. This system must also allow new books to be stored more efficiently without getting lost in the system. Your brain works in a similar way, using complex categories and associations to find hidden information.

Importantly, you are partly responsible for creating this system. Your brain will do a lot for you when you are passive in the process, but you still need to organise your mind if you want your intuition to access information as efficiently as possible. For this reason, I have always found that intuitions are particularly powerful (and accurate) in experts who have developed a strong blueprint for their expertise – a well-practised process which they have applied very deliberately over many years. For instance, take a defence lawyer in court, a surgeon in theatre or a financial trader analysing the markets. Typically, they have experienced similar situations in thousands of subtly different ways, making their subconscious pattern recognition highly nuanced and their intuition highly tuned.

In his classic book *Sources of Power*, psychologist Gary Klein explored the decision making of nurses, intensive care staff and fire-fighters, all of whom regularly have to make decisions under pressure.[2] He discovered that when experts make decisions they don't logically and systematically compare all available options. That's how people are taught to make decisions in the classroom, but in critical moments this is too slow – especially when people's lives are at risk. Instead, they size up a situation almost immediately and act, drawing on a rough mental simulation that comes from their extensive library of experience. From my own familiarity with this idea, I came to realise that this was exactly how military commanders make decisions on the battlefield as well. But, importantly, it takes a lot to get to this point.

Many people think they have good judgement under pressure, but I suspect this is like the 80 per cent of people who think they are better than average at driving a car. The reason I believe front-line forces are often superior at this has little to do with the number of qualifications they have – some of the soldiers in my platoon didn't have a single academic grade to their name. But they were intuitive and could often make very good decisions under pressure, something that, I believe, boils down to their training.

Having gone through this training myself, I learned that the amount of knowledge someone could regurgitate from memory was far less important than the ability to critically analyse a novel situation. In the military this analytical process was imprinted in everyone and it was called the 'combat estimate'. The combat estimate involved taking a complex problem and pulling it apart into its basic elements, establishing facts versus assumptions, identifying essential tasks, coming up with options, selecting the best option and building a plan around it. This process could be applied to anything in life, from starting a business to buying a house.

Using this combat estimate process, we were not allowed to come up with a solution prematurely. Decision making didn't even come into the equation until the problem had first been broken down and assessed in detail. How can you possibly make a decision if you don't truly understand the problem? Yet this is exactly what people do when they confuse 'quick thinking' with 'coming up with the first thing that comes to mind'. This is an untrained response. They might get lucky and come up with a plan that works, but they will almost certainly miss something.

I remember how, when we started learning the combat estimate, it would typically take two hours to mentally run through the process and come up with a course of action. And this was for a simple mission. It was hard work, and never really seemed to get easier because the problems we were training to deal with just got more complicated. But now I appreciate the incredible power of this process, training the mind to notice small details, suspend judgement, explore all options, calculate risk, commit to a course of action and communicate your intent clearly to those around you.

Were Klein's front-line workers taking two hours to systematically work through their own combat estimate when people were screaming in pain or buildings were burning down? No, of course not, at least not consciously. But you can be sure that their decisions and actions were subconsciously affected by the hundreds of hours they had been made to practise their own version of the combat estimate in long-hand format.

If you are thinking that this all sounds very structured and formal, you are right. Because intuition needs an underlying structure to govern the vast database of information it has available to it. Without this trained structure, any deviation of pressure, mood, tiredness or confidence in the moment will throw up different results.

In these front-line professions, learning how to think as part of the mental blueprint starts on day one. This mental scaffolding is supplemented over time by knowledge and experience. Not many other professions have a formal process for training critical analysis as a base skill. Instead, many professions are unfortunately trained and assessed on 'what they know', not 'how to think'.

Building your intuitive 'library'

So how can you actually create and store information that may be useful to you at a later date, even if you never consciously realise it? This was brilliantly demonstrated by the England rugby team during their preparations for the 2003 World Cup, which they would go on to win. Their physical preparation may have been done on the sports field, but much of their mental preparation and planning was done in a classroom. In particular they used a technique called War Gaming, which originates from elite military forces and is used by governments and emergency services. Using a clock, a map of the pitch and a scoreboard to simulate random scenarios on the pitch, the players would discuss exactly what they would do in those situations. Initially, they needed plenty of time to solve complex problems and come up with an agreed course of action, but once they got better and quicker at doing this, it started to pay off on the pitch. They became much better at thinking on their feet, making more intuitive decisions under the physical and mental pressure of live play.

War Gaming is used as a method of training predictability in the way you respond to novel situations. By creating made-up scenarios, individuals and teams have to work through those scenarios, discussing the pros and cons of various courses of action. By doing this in slow time, you start to lay the neural foundations for clearer, more intuitive decision making. Without the fear of consequences or the time pressure to make a rushed decision, you can go back and rework the solution as many times as you need to.

As a team this nurtures a shared intelligence that raises the bar on collective intuition over time. From an individual's perspective, you learn your own mind better; from a team perspective, you can read each other's minds. Even if you never experience that particular situation, you have collectively practised the process of solving problems, making it more likely that you will solve future problems better, faster and more consistently.

Become a skilled observer

There can be no doubt that Wolfgang Amadeus Mozart was a musical genius. He was playing symphonies at the age that most of us were playing with stuffed toys. Between the ages of seven and ten he travelled with his father, Leopold, and his sister, Anne-Marie, to 75 towns in 11 countries, playing and composing music for anyone who would listen. The cost of this trip was huge. His father probably wanted to show off Mozart's undeniable talent while earning some money in the process. But for young Wolfgang, the real value was in meeting and learning from his peers, none of whom could quite believe the ability of this child sensation.

On these journeys around Europe the range of musical experiences he picked up and the musicians he met were priceless for a child his age. Among those peers were Johann Bach, Jiří Benda, Christian Cannabich and George Frideric Handel, to name a few. Mozart had a notebook that he carried around everywhere, jotting down lessons and ideas along the way. No other composer had ever been exposed to this many varieties of music. All of these different musical experiences were absorbed into his musical persona, expanding his intuitive range and allowing the obvious talent to be expressed so completely. That he had the ability and application to process these experiences in extraordinary detail made the opportunity even more valuable to him and it undoubtedly contributed to him becoming one of the most celebrated composers of all time. This speaks brilliantly to the Huxley quotation mentioned in the Thinking Dimension: 'Experience is not what happens to a man; it is what a man does with what happens to him.'

Mozart's story is a neat example of how skilled observation is critical for developing our intuitive library, allowing us to embed the wisdom of other people's experience in a profound way that no textbook can possibly teach us. That's because textbooks don't give us the cues that our intuitive brain needs – the sights, the sounds, the movements, the smells and the intensity that embody the depth of real life.

This makes observation one of the most useful yet underutilised practices for building expert intuition. In my view, many professions would make significant performance gains by prioritising the principles of quality observation. I also notice that we stop looking for the opportunity to observe once we are beyond formal learning and we have become 'good enough'. I have been guilty of this myself, yet when I do get around to arranging a number of pure observation days – with either clients or skilled practitioners – I always reap the benefits and end up wondering why I don't do it more often!

We are also hard-wired to learn from other people thanks to a subset of motor neurons in the brain named mirror neurons. These are specialist neurons that not only become activated when we perform an action but also activate when we see someone else performing the same action. Thus, these neurons 'mirror' other people and create a basis of learning from observation. Neuroscientists such as Marco Iacoboni from UCLA have argued that mirror neuron systems in the human brain help us understand the actions and intentions of other people.[3]

So what makes observation more skilled? Observation needs to be much more than just watching someone else or a video of yourself. It's about watching with intent to understand and experience what's going on. Skilled observation incorporates the tactics, techniques, emotions and thoughts of the situation being observed. This takes much more effort but enriches the layers of connections you need to build your intuitive library. To get the most from observation you may need to focus on one particular element at a time. For instance, if you are observing a great public speaker, you may want to focus separately on their body language, their voice, their content.

Of course, there will come a time when you have to practise for yourself to hone the skill, but you shouldn't underestimate the jump-start that observation gives you. It's my experience that we don't generally carve out the time to do this well, if at all. When was the last time you dedicated yourself to learning through watching other people? What made you stop doing this?

Needless to say, if you can observe world-class performers, you will develop a better reference point for your intuition. Don't be afraid to ask questions either, such as 'What made you decide to do that?', 'What were you trying to do?' or 'Would you have done it differently in different circumstances?'

Intuitive learning requires an open and curious mind, so create space and have fun with it. If you are under time pressure or feel under pressure to learn, this will limit your experience. Take proper time out for observation – the investment is worth it.

Too busy to get better

When I started applying the principles of sport psychology more broadly to business, I had the opportunity to work with a national bus company. This company had depots around the country collectively servicing thousands of bus routes. I was delivering a leadership programme for the 20 or so depot managers. They were all excited to be there, as the company had never previously invested so much in their development and they clearly wanted to make the most of the opportunity. They were all motivated to become the best depot managers they could be.

I was curious that, although they all did the same job, they seemed to go about it in completely different ways. Talking to them, it become evident that as a peer group they never spent time with one another. They never visited one another's depots and therefore were limited to their own narrow view of what good looked like. When I suggested that they take a day out to go and spend it in another depot, they looked back at me with horror: 'We can't possibly do that – we are far too busy!'

They were evidently consumed by the churn of everyday activities and deadlines; they were literally running to a timetable. But this in itself presents many potential issues, especially for leaders who really need to keep their heads up, not down. It becomes too easy to use the excuse of 'being busy' as justification for not getting better. And this seems to be truer now than it ever has been.

With this particular group, I managed to integrate peer observation into the programme in order to give them the permission they were looking for. In addition, we came up with specific guidelines to enable them to get the most from their opportunity to observe each other. When they presented back to the executive team at the end of the programme, they almost unanimously said that the opportunity to observe their peers had been the most transformational component of the programme. It's hopefully something they have continued to do ever since.

Reflection

For so many professionals looking to enhance their skills and abilities, training has become something that they are expected to do 'on the job', which implicitly suggests that serving the organisation today is more important than learning for tomorrow. This limits their opportunity for deliberate and focused practice where quality time is taken to reflect, understand and join the dots on their observations and experiences.

One simple technique can go a long way in helping to close this gap: reflection. Consider just how many of us go about our day on autopilot, in essence half asleep and often unaware of what's going on inside and around us. There's a stark consequence to life on autopilot – you risk missing vital opportunities. Opportunities to learn from a project, to try your hand at something new, to contribute to an important decision, to speak up for yourself, to support someone else in their work ... The list goes on.

Opportunities to learn and be inspired are all around you, but you have to be receptive to them. Importantly, this removes the need for repetition as a rather clumsy way of gaining experience, especially in industries where repetition is not a luxury you have. Surgeons may have to operate on a completely novel problem. Lawyers are having to apply old law in modern ways to issues that didn't even exist when they were training. So, if we are only ever immersed in the immediacy of the issues directly in front of us, we are reactive but never adaptive. Because of instantaneous communication, instant access to 24-hour news and information, and a growing addiction to social media, we are processing as much information in one day as our ancestors did in a lifetime. This can leave us incoherent, impatient and wanting more.

Similar to meditation, reflective thinking takes practice. It requires you to slow down, to pause and to reduce information input. The process of reflection helps you make sense of your day-to-day experiences. It can help you to move forward, to come to decisions, to create a course of action, and to challenge yourself to temporarily switch off autopilot and your habitual ways of doing and thinking. When you reflect, you are your own teacher. Through reflection you bring consciousness to something you already know (at the subconscious level), providing you with the insight to teach yourself.

To do it well, it's important to allocate at least 10–15 minutes for reflection a few times a week in an environment that supports you. You should be away from your desk and computer, and in a positive state of mind. I remember working with the CEO of a large organisation who would take himself off to a secret location with a notebook and pen. Nothing else. Sometimes he would be there for 10 minutes, sometimes for two hours, but he always said it was the most important time of his day. What's more, his team all remarked on how much more coherent his communication and behaviour were as a result. This makes reflection a small habit with huge value.

21

Feel: training your physical intuition

Given the nature of this book, it would be foolish of me not to talk about intuition as a physical attribute as well as a mental attribute. Intuition doesn't just exist on an intellectual level; it also shows up in our ability to learn and repeat highly complex skills on autopilot. This is essential for athletes, musicians, nurses, soldiers, pilots and many other professions. Technically, it's the same mechanism at work, whereby you are tapping into your subconscious pattern recognition of a skill, but this form of intuition has some interesting implications for the way you train your skills in the first place.

To illustrate this point, meet Dr Tom Amberry. Dr Amberry just so happens to be a sport psychologist, which, if anything, strengthens the validity of this story. He holds an impressive world record for scoring the most consecutive free throws in basketball without missing. Before I tell you how many, bear in mind that a professional player will typically score about 8 out of 10 baskets from the free-throw line. So if I told you that Dr Amberry scored a whopping 2,750 baskets without missing, you will probably be as stunned as I was on first learning that! In fact, he never actually missed one – the reason he had to stop was because his time was up on court and he got kicked off. Amazingly, Tom was 68 years old at the time and it took him over 12 hours to complete this feat. When was the last time you even stood up for 12 hours, let alone repeated the same repetitive movement for that long? Despite the mental and physical fatigue he undoubtedly endured, his skill never wavered, not once.

So what was his secret? Tom's capacity to repeat exactly the same skill over and over again relied on a technique called analogy learning. This is when rather than trying to break your technique down into smaller parts, you focus on a simple feeling that's more intuitive. For example, if you are taking a golf shot you may imagine simply swinging your arms like a pendulum. By maintaining your focus on a simple and familiar feeling like this, it creates space for your intuition to coordinate the detailed aspects of your muscle movement and rhythm. The alternative is to try to consciously control every aspect of the swing – an approach that opens us up to all sorts of inconsistencies. In Tom's case, he was imagining his left hand reaching into the cookie jar that he had placed on his kitchen shelf at home while imagining his right arm, the shooting arm, extending 15 feet into the air to place the ball in the basket. By refining these 'feelings' he was able to recreate the exact same movement and therefore the exact same outcome every time.

A lot of what allows you to perform on autopilot depends on how you learned the skill in the first place. A golf swing is a good example of this. If you have been taught with a very instructional approach where the skill is broken down into smaller parts, then with practice these smaller parts 'chunk' together to become intuitive. The problem with this type of learning is that under pressure when you really want to 'get it right', the skill can break back down again as you try to take conscious control. In sport psychology we call this reinvestment, because the brain is trying to micro-manage skills that have previously been automated. This causes your technique to actually regress to a less skilled version. You lose fluidity and form, making mistakes far more likely. Of course, the more you are aware of your poor form and fluidity, the more you try to control your technique, further compounding the problem.

Internalising your knowledge and skill

For decades, coaches have tended towards providing step-by-step instructions for developing a skill – we call this explicit learning. In theory this works fine and has an obvious logic to it. The problem is that it is difficult to build true consistency and feel when there are so many moving parts. You are always trying to remember and refine multiple sub-skills, and since one sub-skill might impact many others, it becomes difficult to ring-fence the part of your technique giving you problems. The whole process becomes an intellectual and analytical one at the very point it needs to be intuitive. As a result, when an explicit learner gets tired and loses concentration, they will lean towards trying to control even more rather than letting go and keeping things simple.

This type of explicit learning I also call Outside-In learning because the technique is monitored and corrected from the outside. Without external measurements and feedback the performer has no idea how they are doing. However, implicit learning, or Inside-Out learning, is much more reliant on the learner having an internal blueprint for what good feels like. More than this, their blueprint is stable and consistent within their mind. It has been practised and there is an easy route back to it. Neurologically, this means that a single point of focus (such as a hand in the cookie jar) can give you consistent access to a complex system of pathways within the brain, with far less conscious thought or effort than if you had learned the skill explicitly.

Interestingly, this leads to a very different approach to how we correct our mistakes. Following a mistake, an Outside-In learner may ask: 'What did I do wrong?' The answer to that exists somewhere within a long list of instructions telling them what the 'correct' process is. An implicit or Inside-Out learner would ask: 'What should good feel like?' The answer to this is always the same: 'My internalised blueprint.' This mental model offers total consistency and is more resilient to fatigue, overthinking and outside interference.

This approach was brilliantly illustrated in one of my fondest experiences as a performance psychologist. It came about early in my career when I was asked to work with a four-man rowing crew from Vesta Rowing Club in London. This ambitious and committed team were preparing to compete at Henley Royal Regatta, the oldest and most prestigious rowing regatta in the world. The club itself had never reached the final stages of the regatta, and simply qualifying would be an achievement for this particular crew.

I remember first asking each of the rowers to write a short essay describing their perfect race along the 2-kilometre (1.2-mile) course in as much detail as they could. I realised that getting them to write a short essay would probably make me unpopular from the outset, but I was keen to understand how they all defined success in their minds. When I asked them to read their essays out loud to the rest of the team and the coach, it became evident that they were all internalising a different race in their head, and some were less clear than others. I then asked them to use what they had written to come up with a collective 'best'. With a few heated discussions along the way, this became their mental blueprint, which we would end up measuring our progress against.

Next they learned the Three Foundations, visualising their collective blueprint as their positive focus, or at least small chunks of it. We tried to make every aspect of the race as real as possible in their minds, so to help bring their visualised experience to life we enlisted a DJ to create a mix of music that lasted the exact duration of their best imagined race. The focus of the race was split naturally into thirds, each with a slightly different emphasis on rhythm, length of stroke, power and intensity. The music was designed to represent each section. After opening with 'Children' by Robert Miles, the mix continued until finishing with something more euphoric and intense for the final strokes.

Alongside their physical training sessions, the rowers also worked on their visualisation. Eventually, they were able to mentally rehearse the whole race in real time with perfect form. At this point I knew they were ready for their final challenge: to do a time trial on the rowing machines while blindfolded!

I would be lying if I told you that they jumped at this opportunity; in fact, I remember a great deal of resistance coming back at me. This is understandable because rowers rely on getting good times from these tests as a measure of their progress. If we messed around and caused them to get a bad time, they might lose confidence. But here's the thing: if we are relying on data as the only source of feedback to tell us how we are doing there is a danger that our natural, internalised 'feel' gets eroded by the numbers on a screen. The constant analysis and self-editing that comes from asking questions like 'How am I doing?' and 'How should I be doing?' destroys this intuitive feel at the point where we should simply be focused on the plan that we had visualised. The moment you are using external feedback to make sense of your internal experience you are walking down the path of inconsistency.

In reality we didn't actually do it blindfolded; instead, we just taped the screens up on the rowing machines so that the rowers couldn't read the data. We also played the music out loud which had now been anchored to their blueprint. Without any feedback from the screen telling them how fast they were going or how much distance they had covered, the music helped them to tap into their intuitive feel for the race.

Regardless of what they would go on to achieve at Henley, the result of that time trial made it all worth it as far as I was concerned. Three out of the four rowers smashed their personal best times. Two of them said they didn't even believe they were capable of the times they got. So the big question is, would they have got those times if they had been staring at a screen?

Henley rolled on and the team achieved their initial goal by qualifying as a wild card. This would have been cause for celebration in itself beforehand, but now there was an Inside-Out confidence in what they were capable of. In the opening round of the knock-out competition, they were drawn against one of the top-seeded crews who had travelled all the way from Sydney to compete. It was a shock to many when the Vesta crew beat the Australians in the first round. They continued through the regatta, beating teams who, on paper, were far superior. The team responded to every challenge impeccably along the way. Just before one of their races, the wind was so strong they had to sit on the start line for 10 minutes. They all knew exactly what to do and how to refocus on their job when the moment came.

Speaking to them during the week of racing, I noticed that they were never concerned who their opponents were. They also weren't analysing the scoreboard or comparing times; they were simply focused on repeating the quality of their own race – every time. They knew that, if they did that, they would have done everything they could. By the time the crew arrived at the semi-finals on the Saturday, the banks were filled with thousands of spectators all the way along the course. The team won their race, making it through to the final day of the regatta.

They would end up losing by just half a length to the tournament's top-seeded crew. It was a phenomenal performance that gained the admiration of some bewildered pundits. But more than that, the team had learned how to internalise excellence to recreate their best every time, no matter what the external conditions or who their opponents were.

22
Flow: the elusive state of peak performance

At the beginning of this book, I wrote about a transformational experience I had during an international modern pentathlon competition in Cairo. It was there that I discovered the elusive state of 'flow'. Flow gives us unbridled access to our trained subconscious. I have had similar experiences since, although none quite as undiluted as that. It was as though all my senses coalesced to become one, with a singular point of focus guiding everything I did. I was totally in control – but without having to work at being in control. I was 100 per cent in the moment and never once considered 'How am I doing?' in the context of the competition.

I appreciate that the description of flow can sound a little nebulous, but that's partly because it's impossible to describe in words what is primarily an intuitive and sensory experience. The name 'flow' was coined by Hungarian psychologist Mihaly Csikszentmihalyi in the 1970s.[1] He described it as 'a deeply rewarding and optimal experience characterised by intense focus on a specific activity to the point of becoming totally absorbed in it'. For obvious reasons it's often a favourite topic for performance psychologists – the holy grail of mental performance. You may have experienced being in flow yourself at some point, perhaps while doing an activity you loved or a task you were well skilled at.

The flow state is somewhat of a paradox. I had always approached training, both sport and military, with the utmost structure, logic and control. Yet this experience, paradoxically, felt detached, timeless and effortless. It was like my conscious mind had simply excused itself, having done all the work to get there, stepping aside for my subconscious to take charge. Many people have likened flow to an out-of-body experience, so it's no wonder that in some cultures flow is also called *ecstasis*, from the Greek word for 'ecstasy', meaning to stand outside oneself. It seems that, despite all the hard work and conscious planning that get us to the moment of peak performance, our intuition can only truly be expressed through our ability to let go and perform with freedom.

Importantly, one of the essential ingredients for achieving flow is the ability to detach yourself from the outcome of what you do. This is exceptionally difficult to achieve, not least if you have invested time, effort and emotional energy getting as far as you have. Ironically, this makes flow easier to achieve when you are in a state of playfulness than when you are hungry for results, which explains why flow states are particularly elusive during high-pressure events. But not impossible! Get this right and you should be able to perform with total freedom – whatever the circumstances, whoever is watching, whatever the consequences.

So what's going on in the brain and body while this is happening, and can this give you any clues as to how you might be able to better induce these peak performance states? The fascinating thing about flow, as distinct from a coherent state, is its unique profile of brain activity. For a start, at the point when you are in flow there is less activity in areas of the prefrontal cortex responsible for awareness of time, complex decisions, worrying about the future and self-judgement.

In particular, with less awareness of time due to reduced temporal processing in the brain, you have no reference point for past, present and future. This effectively plunges you into an elongated present, described by researchers as 'the deep now'. Energy normally used for temporal processing gets reallocated for attention and focus. You take in more data per second and process it more deeply. This creates the illusion that the moment is lasting longer. At the same time, the more neurotic, reactive parts of the brain shut down, reducing any sensations of fight-or-flight.

Flow state can also significantly boost creativity and problem solving. Researchers at the University of Sydney managed to induce flow states in participants using a transcranial magnetic stimulation machine.[2] They were then given 10 minutes to complete the

nine-dot problem, connecting nine dots with four lines without lift-
ing the pencil from the paper. In the control group, not a single
participant completed the task (you would normally expect 5 per
cent of the population to be successful). In the flow-induced group, a
massive 40 per cent were successful, and in record time.

In similar studies conducted with the US military, flow-induced
soldiers solved complex problems and mastered new skills up to 490
per cent faster than normal. Global consultancy McKinsey also concluded, following a 10-year global study of companies, that top executives were up to 500 per cent more productive in flow.[3]

In the Feeling Dimension we explored the process of practising
coherent states as part of our day-to-day training. In particular, we
used the Three Foundations of deep breathing, active relaxation and
positive focus as a way of training a coherent state. A coherent state is
a precursor to flow, but it is not flow itself. Flow is a deeper and more
elusive state that is less within our control. Therefore, flow becomes
an output, not an input, meaning that you shouldn't put yourself
under pressure to achieve flow. That said, with extensive practice,
preparation and the appropriate level of challenge, flow is more likely
to happen. Flow is something you tend to talk about after the event
rather than obsess about beforehand, whereas breathing, relaxation
and focus might well feature in your process goals prior to an event.

Importantly, flow can be achieved only when your skill level
matches the challenge. If the task is too hard, your concentration
suffers because your working memory is overstretched as you struggle to grapple with the task. Too easy and your working memory is
underutilised, so your attentional resources are likely to be divided.
The trick is being able to set yourself challenges and goals that perfectly match the attentional resources (or 'processing power') you
have available. Under pressure, your attentional capacity will be
restricted as resources get reallocated to feed your heightened senses.
This is why, in competition, athletes do well to keep their goals far
more simple than they might do in training. This will not diminish
their performance in any way since their conscious focus is merely
the window into their far more powerful subconscious. And it's the
trained subconscious that does most of the work.

If my own experiences of flow states taught me anything, it was the need to be extremely confident in yourself and your process. If you are too self-conscious, worrying about what other people are doing or about what they might think, then flow becomes impossible. Peak performance states are synonymous with a high level of expertise, but it's not enough to simply have the ability. You need to own your environment and feel like you belong there for expertise to translate into flow. This is relevant to some of the principles we covered in the chapters on belief and identity, which you may find useful to re-read.

Team flow

Although it lies beyond the remit of this book, which focuses more on personal performance, flow can also be achieved as a collective. In the same way that flow state is a proxy for mastery at an individual level, it is also a proxy for mastery at a team level, which is far harder to achieve.

Nowhere is this better demonstrated than in the SAS's 'Kill House', the rather candid name given to their indoor training facility designed for hostage-rescue simulations. Conditions in this environment are immensely challenging. For a start, the soldiers often have to conduct their missions in the dark while wearing respirators which narrow their field of vision. Every gunshot and grenade creates deafening blasts which can be extremely disorienting. In these situations, it's not enough to be able to manage yourself; success requires an almost superhuman collective awareness of those around you. If the person in front looks left, you need to look right. Whoever knows what to do next becomes the leader. This could be anyone based on circumstance. The moment someone steps up, the team must immediately trust that person and, without second-guessing, move with them.

Navy SEALs call this 'dynamic subordination', where leadership is fluid and defined by conditions on the ground. It requires complete mastery and trust of every sub-skill that brought them to that moment in time, from weapon-handling drills to communication to observation. Done well, it's an awesome force, a team moving as one at breakneck speed through a building, their brains intuitively mapping out each room and the relative positions of everyone around them.

Whether working as an individual or as a team, flow requires structure and discipline. Without the micro-skills, rehearsed routines and standard operating procedures that underpin your blueprint for success, you are likely to find little other than chaos in a highly charged environment. It's an important reminder that peak performance requires you to work hard on your mental and physical routines in order to guide your autopilot.

Flow and meaning

Finally, it is impossible to separate flow states from the profound sense of meaning and enjoyment that you get from doing what you love. Therefore it seems apt to leave my final words on flow to the master of flow research himself, Mihaly Csikszentmihalyi:

> Meaning, substance, real enjoyment in life comes in just improving performance, not by winning or setting records. Enjoyment is in the process of improvements and self-mastery. However we need a goal – perhaps of being first – or we don't stretch ourselves. It is good to have a realistic goal and a commitment to achieving it, but also to know that the end goal is not all there is. The process is what counts.

> What we are talking about with flow and performance, really, is happiness. Happiness depends on what you do, the use of your skills, overcoming challenges, being sensitive to your environment, to what is unfolding, but not trying to control the environment or forcing yourself on it. It is adapting to changes, doing your best, and not worrying about the outcome.

> This is freedom. You drop selfish goals and do your best, whatever happens. You surrender to the process.

Final thoughts: applying *Inside Out* to your *world*

'What lies behind us and what lies before us are tiny
matters compared to what lies within us.'

Oliver Wendell Holmes

Inside Out is for all of us

There are two statements that I work hard to avoid people ever having to say.

1 'This stuff is for the pros, not for the amateurs.'

This is simply not true. I have worked at every single level of sport, business and the military, from people starting out to those who are number one in the world. In terms of mental training, I don't consider my approach any different at either end of the spectrum. Excellence is an attitude, not a skill; therefore it can be applied on every rung of the ladder.

If you are saying, 'Other amateurs don't do this', then that is a very different statement. It implies you have a choice. And trust me, when the pros were in your shoes, they were the ones who stood out and made that choice. That's why they are now pros.

2 'I wish I knew then what I know now.'

There will naturally be an evolution in our understanding of what it takes to be great at what we do, especially when industries such as sport science are constantly looking to push our knowledge and boundaries of human performance. However, there is nothing worse than the regret of knowing that you could have done something better.

Therefore, take the opportunity while you have it. If there are parts of this book that really resonate with you, commit to making them part of your approach and who you are – today.

Make Inside Out part of your everyday

You might be curious as to how many of the core techniques described in this book, such as breathing, visualisation, self-analysis and skilled observation, are adhered to by high performers. And it's a fair question. I'm afraid the answer is exceptionally vague – most of them adhere to most of the techniques.

The reality of it is that, given the time, money and energy, there is plenty that every elite performer could get better at if they took time to audit their performance playbook. Do SAS troops use visualisation as a deliberate part of their mental process? Many of them, yes, and far more now than used to. But it doesn't define what it means to be an SAS soldier. Like every professional group, there are some who take it very seriously, others who recognise the value of it enough to practise it while queuing at the supermarket or in the gym, and then others who don't give it a second thought. In this regard the question could just as easily be: 'Do primary school teachers visualise?' or 'Do actors visualise?' It depends more on the person than it does on the job, though for a combat soldier the intensity of the job and the consequences of poor mind–body management are undoubtedly more severe.

What I would say about Special Forces soldiers is that, whether they realise it or not, they all have their own rituals and techniques for managing the mental and physiological aspects of their job. So long as those rituals are based on sound principles, it should work well for them. While not all Special Forces soldiers visualise, I've yet to meet one who doesn't at least apply the principle on some level to how they mentally and physically prepare. They also seem to be hugely respectful and open-minded towards one another's individual performance routines. Anything that helps their teammates find their own state of excellence is a good thing for them.

The ones who take time to develop and practise the techniques that work for them are the ones who generally maintain high levels of personal effectiveness and therefore often the ones who go further. Similarly, it is commonplace for athletes, surgeons and musicians to adopt unique rituals before they perform.

By taking a more deliberate approach to mental training, it can transform the personal effectiveness of every single one of us.

Live a more fulfilling life

When I first sat down to write this book, I wanted it to be about more than personal achievement and winning. I believe that some of the ideas discussed in this book have profound implications for living a life more fulfilled.

I remember when I had my first paid job in sport psychology, working at Whitgift School in Croydon, London. I spent three very happy years there and was given the freedom to practise and try new things while helping kids get better at their sport. I suspect some of the mental skills and practices I had them doing were quite unorthodox, but, none the wiser, they embraced them with the same enthusiasm that they did any other part of their sport. More than anything, I wanted them to understand that their mind was the most important tool they had in life – but they had to nourish it.

Ten years later it filled me with joy when I saw one of these boys, Joseph Choong, fulfil his dream of winning a gold medal at the 2020 Tokyo Olympics. As if this wasn't remarkable enough, on the very same day that Joe was winning his gold medal in Tokyo, Saturday, 7 August 2021, two other boys in that original school group were realising their own sporting dreams. Elliot Daly was playing for the British Lions against South Africa in Cape Town and Dom Sibley was opening the batting for the England cricket team against India. Their talent and hard work as younger boys was unquestionable, but their collective achievement across such diverse sports is also a wonderful example of how powerful it is to embed sound psychological principles into training and competition from an early age. Despite these accolades, what I enjoyed the most was receiving a letter from one of them soon after I left the school, thanking me for helping him achieve the grades he needed to get into university. At no point had we ever discussed academic work – but it turned out he had been so anxious about failing his exams that he was applying the same mental skills we had used on the training field. For me, there couldn't be a better example of how sport is the ultimate playground for life.

It may feel messy – embrace the funk

Behind any inspiring story is a messy reality. When the outcome is good, it's easy to reminisce on how everything else was good, too – how everyone did their job and everything went to plan. Even the most successful experiences I've had with individuals and teams were coupled with extremely hard work, difficult challenges, strained relationships and tough conversations, most of which get forgotten at the point of victory. I believe it's important to remember these challenging moments, not because you want them to happen again but because they *will* happen again. It's simply part of the process, and if high performance were easy, it would no longer be high performance!

When you're in the midst of it and you don't know how the story's going to end, it can feel relentless and scary. Sometimes you forget the lessons you need to make you wiser and stronger when the time comes to do it again. It's important that you are able to 'clean up' important lessons from your experience so that you can go forward with confidence and clarity, but relationships are complex, competitors are relentless, and when you are pushing your limits, everyone will make mistakes. All of these things create a cocktail of discomfort which can, at times, feel overwhelming. As if you're never going to get this right.

Even when results are going your way there will always be something to look out for, something not quite as it should be. I now realise this is normal, and for anyone who finds themselves embarking on a competitive career, perhaps entering the arena of high performance for the first time, I encourage you to embrace the funk of it and be

conscious of how you choose to respond to the toughest moments –
lean into them, speak the truth, but be kind, recognise every small win,
find time to laugh and put things into perspective, then get your head
back down again.

Focus on certainty, not uncertainty

I'm convinced that 90 per cent of business blogs lead with the sentiment that the world is more uncertain than it has ever been. I
wouldn't dare to disagree with this, but I hope that after reading this
book you will agree with me when I say that, by talking about all
the uncertainty that exists around us, we are focusing on the wrong
thing. I believe that, as well as there being more uncertainty than ever
before, there is also as much certainty as there has ever been.

To explain this riddle, imagine I sent you to the shop to buy some
salad dressing. You might consider the task to be fairly straightforward
– until you stand there in front of the shelf faced with 20 varieties of
salad dressing. Now what seemed like a fairly simple task has become
full of uncertainty as you struggle to weigh up the hundreds of factors for making the perfect decision – price, what's on offer, size of
bottle, what flavour I might like, and so on. We've all experienced this
moment of paralysis. But for me you are not dealing with the challenge of uncertainty, you are dealing with the challenge of choice.
The moment you make a decision, uncertainty miraculously trans-
forms into certainty. It turns out that uncertainty had nothing to do
with 'the world' around you and everything to do with your ability to
make clear choices and decisions. Despite this, it will always be much
easier to blame conditions on the outside.

This helps explain why one of the most persistent traits I have
noticed in high performers is their ability and desire to create their
own certainty. This says a lot in a world where we have more choice
than ever. Consider an entrepreneur starting their own business –
they have more ways of generating revenue than ever before, more
ways of spending money, raising money, marketing their business,
manufacturing their product, employing staff and so on.

When a potential investor decides they don't want to fund your new business, this isn't up to you. But the decision to improve your pitch? That is. This working revolution is both a blessing and a curse, depending on how you are able to deal with choice.

Your mind is amazing

Most of all, I want you to remember how amazing your mind is. Like many of life's precious resources, we have come to notice our mind only when something goes wrong. The mind is easy to take for granted and easy to neglect, especially when you are wired to the outside world 24/7. You are used to an omnipresent, low level of stress that makes you believe you are busy, when actually you are just vacant, with reduced capacity to think and feel.

As much as your mind has the capacity to torment you, it can also deliver you immense joy, satisfaction and fulfilment when you are facing in the right direction. My intention for this book is not simply to tell you how important your mind is, it is also to encourage you to practise using it in different ways. If you nurture it, challenge it and rest it, it will give back more than you could ever know.

Own your performance – do it *your* way

The Tokyo Olympic Games will forever be remembered as the 'COVID Olympics' – the Games with no crowd. But it will also be remembered for the Games in which competitors started to speak openly about the challenges they faced on the inside as well as the outside. I was the mental coach for some of these athletes, and for me it reinforced the importance of mental health as well as mental performance, with the inner workings of top names like Simone Biles laid bare for everyone to see. I find myself questioning how it got to this point and what we can do to address the root cause much earlier.

The need to live up to other people's expectations is also a strong part of the equation for many of these athletes. They are not just representing their own ambitions but also the ambitions of their coaches and their wider team. Young people especially must be given help to shape their own story in a way that is authentic and real for them, so that they are not coerced into trying to live out a narrative that is shaped by their external world and the media. If we are trying to live up to other people's version of our story, then we will start to self-edit in a way that inhibits our freedom to perform. To be at our best we must be ourselves with skill. But this needs working at (and stress-testing) well before the immersive pressure of an Olympic Games.

All of this comes as a striking reminder that, for me, I do not really work with athletes in this context. I work with human beings. For all of us who are responsible for working with other people's hopes and dreams, we will always do well to remember this.

I started this book in Cairo, and it's there I would like to end – with the perfect five shots that followed an expected disruption at the back of the shooting hall. I can say with some certainty that in these last five shots of the competition I didn't shoot five 'centre tens' *in spite* of the fight at the back of the hall. I shot them *because* of it.

In the unplanned 10 minutes between the Egyptian and the Russian coaches being removed from the hall, most athletes were simply trying to stay composed, walking around, sipping water. I was back in my kitchen at home running through the same calm, focused process I always had done – one breath relaxation, one breath visualisation, calm, control, sights. One breath relaxation, one breath visualisation, calm, control, sights … and so on. Through familiar repetition, there came a point when every part of my mind–body system became 'locked in' to this rhythm. In doing so, my actions on the outside became close to identical to the visualised experience on the inside.

This small but important part of my story helped me to recognise and appreciate a similar story in others. Most of what you require to perform at your best you have inside – a wealth of resources that goes largely untapped. Why does it go untapped? Partly because you don't make mental training part of your process in the first place, but more significantly because you are scared about changing your habits and routines for fear of standing out from the crowd.

Many people have grown up learning to protect their inner world from their outer world – to expose it would make them vulnerable. Don't be afraid to try your absolute best. You will never be close to your actual best by pretending that you don't care. This is akin to the parents' race on school sports day – you want to win but you don't want to be seen trying too hard. That's probably okay for the parents' race, but if you go through life protecting your ego from the fear of losing or looking silly, you will never create the opportunity to explore your true potential.

There is a comfort in the things you have always done, even if they don't deliver the best results for you. You must overcome this if you want to explore your best – and the first step is to simply give yourself permission to try hard.

Everything you have practised has got you to this point. You won't be able to bring it all to mind at once, but you don't need to. It's in you. You are here, now, and you are ready. As you approach the start line, walk into the exam hall, stand up on stage to address the audience, you need only do three things: breathe deeply, relax into it, and focus on your process, one step at a time. Trust your training. Trust your process. Trust yourself. Trust … and go!

References

Chapter 1

1 Mark Williams and Tim Wigmore, *The Best: How Elite Athletes Are Made* (John Murray Press, 2020).
2 Frank Sulloway and Richard Zweigenhaft, 'Birth order and risk taking in athletics: A meta-analysis and study of Major League baseball', *Personality and Social Psychology Review* 14.4 (November 2010).
3 Ed Smith, *What Sport Teaches Us about Life* (Penguin, 2008).

Chapter 2

1 Carol Dweck, *The New Psychology of Success* (Ballantine Books, 2007).

Chapter 4

1 Jeffrey A. Gray and Neil McNaughton, 'The neuropsychology of anxiety: An enquiry into the function of the septo-hippocampal system', Oxford Scholarship Online (January 2008).
2 W. Helton and J. Head, 'Earthquakes on the mind: Implications of disasters for human performance', *Human Factors* 54 (2012): 189–94.

Chapter 6

1 Ian McGregor, Kyle A. Nash and Michael Inzlicht, 'Threat, high self-esteem, and reactive approach-motivation: Electroencephalographic

evidence', *Journal of Experimental Social Psychology* 45.4 (2009): 1003–7.

2 Ian Robertson, *The Stress Test* (Bloomsbury Publishing, 2016).

Chapter 7

1 Malcolm Gladwell, *Outliers* (Penguin, 2008).

Chapter 10

1 Antoine Lutz, Lawrence L. Greischar, Nancy B. Rawlings, Mattieu Ricard and Richard J. Davidson, 'Long-term meditators self-induce high amplitude gamma synchrony during mental practice', *Proceedings of the National Academy of Science* 101.46 (2004): 16369–73.

Chapter 11

1 Philippe R. Goldin, Kateri McRae, Wiveka Ramel and James J. Gross, 'The neural basis of emotion regulation: reappraisal and suppression of negative emotion', *Biological Psychiatry* 63.6 (2008): 577–86.

Chapter 13

1 A. St Clair Gibson et al., 'Regulatory, integrative and comparative physiology', *American Journal of Physiology* (2001): 281.

2 Timothy David Noakes et al., 'Evidence that a central governor regulates exercise performance during acute hypoxia and hyperoxia', *The Journal of Experimental Biology* 204 (2001): 3225–34.

3 Timothy David Noakes, 'Time to move beyond a brainless exercise physiology: The evidence for complex regulation of human exercise performance', *Applied Physiology, Nutrition and Metabolism* 36 (2011): 23–5.

4 Charlie Wells and Lisa Fleisher, 'How to survive an 80-hour work week'. *Bloomberg Wealth*, 25 March 2021, available at: www.bloomberg.com/news/newsletters/2021-03-25/bloomberg-wealth-how-to-survive-an-80-hour-work-week.

5 K Gilchrist, 'Microsoft Japan 4-hour work week experiment sees productivity jump 40 percent', CNBC, 3 November 2019, available at: www.cnbc.com/2019/11/04/microsoft-japan-4-day-work-week-experiment-sees-productivity-jump-40percent.html.

6 Owen Jones, 'Four-day week: Trial finds lower stress and increased productivity', *Guardian*, 19 February 2019, available at: www.the-guardian.com/money/2019/feb/19/four-day-week-trial-study-finds-lower-stress-but-no-cut-in-output

7 C.W., 'Proof that you should get a life', *The Economist*, 9 December 2014, available at www.economist.com/free-exchange/2014/12/09/proof-that-you-should-get-a-life

Chapter 14

1 All quotes taken from Levan Tsikurishvili (director), *Avicii: True Stories*, Black Dalmatian Films: 27 October 2017.

Chapter 15

1 Alia J. Crum, Peter Salovey and Shawn Achor, 'Rethinking stress: The role of mindsets in determining the stress response', *Journal of Personality and Social Psychology* 104.4 (2013): 716–33.

2 Charles A. Morgan, Steve Southwick, Gary Hazlett, Ann Rasmusson, Gary Hoyt, Zoran Zimolo and Dennis Charney, 'Relationships among plasma dehydroepiandrosterone sulfate and cortisol levels, symptoms of dissociation, and objective performance in humans exposed to acute stress', *The Archives of General Psychology* 61.8 (Aug 2004): 819–25.

Chapter 16

1 Donald G. Dutton and Arthur P. Aron, 'Some evidence for heightened sexual attraction under conditions of high anxiety', *Journal of Personality and Social Psychology* 30.4 (1974): 510.

Chapter 17

1 Daniel Amen, foreword to Deborah Rozman and Rollin McCraty (eds), *HeartMath Brain Fitness Program* (Waterfront Press, 2017).
2 Deborah Rozman and Rollin McCraty, *HeartMath Brain Fitness Program* (Waterfront Press, 2017).

Chapter 18

1 Matthijs Kox, Lucas T. van Eijk, Jelle Zwaag, Joanne van den Wildenberg, Fred C. G. J. Sweep, Johannes G. van der Hoeven and Peter Pickkers, 'Voluntary activation of the sympathetic nervous system and attenuation of the innate immune response in humans', National Library of Medicine: National Centre for Biotechnology Information, 2014, accessed via pubmed.ncbi.nlm.nih.gov/24799686/.

Chapter 19

1 Robert Pirsig, *Zen and the Art of Motorcycle Maintenance* (William Morrow and Company, 1974).

Chapter 20

1 A. Dijksterhuis and A. van Knippenberg, 'The relationship between perception and behaviour, or how to win a game of Trivial Pursuit', *Journal of Personality and Social Psychology* 74.4 (1998): 797–811.
2 Gary Klein, *Sources of Power* (MIT Press, 2018).
3 Marco Iacoboni, 'The mirror neuron revolution: Explaining what makes humans social', an interview for *Scientific American* (2008).

Chapter 22

1 Mihaly Csikszentmihalyi, *Flow* (Harper & Row, 1990).
2 Richard Chi and Allan Snyder, 'Brain stimulation enables solution to inherently difficult problem', *Neuroscience Letters* 515 (2012): 121–4.

3 Susie Cranston and Scott Keller, 'Increasing the "meaning quotient" of work', *McKinsey Quarterly*, 1 January 2013, available at www.mckinsey.com/business-functions/organization/our-insights/increasing-the-meaning-quotient-of-work.

Index

McNeil, Pablo, 14
meditation, 39, 82–3, 140–2
memory, 80–1
mental aptitude, 3
  connections, 67–76
  feedback, 77–83
  learning, 55–8
  repetition, 59–65
  resonance, 85–92
mental attitude, 3, 5–17
  belief, 41–7
  failure, 25–9
  focus, 31–40
  talent, 19–24
mental blueprint, 70, 71–6, 88,
  142
  A-Days, 148–9
  of front-line professionals, 178
  for implicit learning, 187–9
  overcoming fear, 144
mental fitness, 151–3
mental training, xvi, 146–7
Messi, Lionel, 20
metrics, as measure of success,
  11–13
Microsoft, 105
mindset, 3, 5–17
  for Intuitive Dimension, 170–1
  response to failure, 28
mini-successes, 29
mirror neurons, 181
modern pentathlon, 115–16
mogul skiing, 89
mood–state congruence, 60
Morgan, Andy, 118, 121
motivation for learning
  psychological techniques, 6
Mozart, Wolfgang Amadeus, 180
Murray, Andy, 9

Murray, Sam, 115
'muscle memory', 60
muscular tension, 135–7
music, in learning process, 188–9
music production, 111–14

natural disasters, stressful effect,
  31–2, 34
negative thinking, 6–8
nervous system, 127–31, 143, 154–7
neural pathways, 7
neurocardiology, 127–31
neuroscience
  of learning, 57–8, 60–1, 181
  making connections, 67–8
  of meditation, 82–3
Noakes, Tim, 102

observation, 180–2
obstacles to success, 17
O'Sullivan, Lt. Luke, 62–3, 78,
  173–5
outcomes
  binary thinking, 29
  as measure of success, 12–15
Outside-In mindset, 12–13
  explicit learning, 186–7
  from an Inside-Out mindset,
    16–17
  response to failure, 28
overthinking, 74–5

panic, 101, 113–14
Parsons, Dominic, 2
penalty taking, 33
Pencavel, John, 105
performance anxiety, 101,
  113–14

About the author

© Lucy Williams Photography

Charlie Unwin was born in Cambridge and brought up on a farm in the Essex/Suffolk countryside. He had an early passion for sport, influenced greatly by his late father, Jim Unwin, who played rugby for England and the British Lions.

Having studied Psychology at Durham University he went on to join the army. He started training at the Royal Military Academy Sandhurst just two days before the planes flew into the Twin Towers. He commissioned into the 1st Regiment Royal Horse Artillery and served in Iraq in 2004. As a 23-year-old platoon commander, he was responsible for a leading counter-insurgency operations in the south of the country as well as helping to recruit and train the new Basra police force.

As an athlete in the sport of Modern Pentathlon, he fulfilled his goal of representing TeamGB at the World Championships in 2015. He also became National Champion in the same year. It was during his time as an athlete that his passion for applied psychology flourished. Whilst gaining a further MSc in Sport Psychology at Brunel University, he won a national postgraduate award for his applied research into the mindset of elite performers. He started to formalise his approach and techniques for working with top athletes and in doing so had the opportunity to apply these principles into other industries. As a performance consultant he has designed award-winning programmes and worked with graduates to senior executives in organisations such as Coca-Cola, Dyson and Lego.

He has delivered training to UK Special Forces (SAS & SBS) and has also delivered masterclasses for organisations like the Bank of England and the Royal Household. In addition he has contributed to the training of elite specialists including fighter pilots, surgeons, lawyers and nuclear scientists. These experiences all reinforced his core belief that the basic principles of human performance are important to anyone who seeks excellence – no matter what they do.

In 2012 he was offered the role of performance psychologist for the GB Skeleton team who went on to become Great Britain's most successful Winter Olympic team of all time. He worked closely with Lizzy Yarnold OBE in her journey to becoming double Olympic Champion and GB's most decorated Winter Olympic athlete.

At the 2020 Tokyo Olympics he worked with athletes across multiple sports who, between them, returned with an impressive haul of four gold medals, three silvers and one bronze.

As a coach mentor Charlie works with Premier League clubs including Arsenal and West Ham. He has also worked with England Football on delivering results under pressure and developing the psychological resilience of players from an early age.

He now lives in the Cotswolds near Bath with his lovely wife Rose, his son Austin and their two spaniels, Rocco and Nelson.

Charlie Unwin is a popular speaker and performance consultant. If you are interested in how he can work with your organisation, please visit www.charlieunwin.com and get in touch.

Would you like your people to read this book?

If you would like to discuss how you could bring these ideas to your team, we would love to hear from you. Our titles are available at competitive discounts when purchased in bulk across both physical and digital formats. We can offer bespoke editions featuring corporate logos, customized covers, or letters from company directors in the front matter can also be created in line with your special requirements.

We work closely with leading experts and organizations to bring forward-thinking ideas to a global audience. Our books are designed to help you be more successful in work and life.

For further information, or to request a catalogue, please contact:
business@johnmurrays.co.uk
sales-US@nicholasbrealey.com (North America only)

Nicholas Brealey Publishing is an imprint of
John Murray Press.